STRAVINSKY

in the theatre

Igor Stravinsky. New York, 1948 (Photograph: Gene Fenn)

STRAVINSKY

IN THE THEATRE

———

Edited with an Introduction by Minna Lederman

A DA CAPO PAPERBACK

Library of Congress Cataloging in Publication Data

Lederman, Minna, ed.
  Stravinsky in the theatre.

  (A Da Capo paperback)
  Reprint of the ed. published by Pellegrini &
Cudahy, New York.
  "Stage productions": p.
  Discography: p.
  Bibliography: p.
  1. Stravinskiĭ, Igor' Fedorovich, 1882-1971.
I. Title.
[ML410.S932L4 1975b]   782.9'5'0924   75-14126
ISBN 0-306-80022-5

First paperback printing 1975
ISBN: 0-306-80022-5

This Da Capo Press edition of *Stravinsky in the Theatre* in an
unabridged republication of the first edition published in
New York in 1949. It is published with the permission of Farrar,
Straus & Giroux, Inc.

Published by Da Capo Press, Inc.
A Subsidiary of Plenum Publishing Corporation
227 West 17th Street, New York, N.Y. 10011

ACKNOWLEDGMENTS

The music quotations used by Messrs. Ansermet, Balanchine, Berger, Craft and Dahl are reproduced by permission of the following copyright owners:

Boosey and Hawkes, Inc.,—*Petrouchka, Piano Concerto, Apollon Musagètes, Le Sacre du Printemps, Orpheus, Mass, Symphonie de Psaumes, Oedipus Rex, Le Rossignol, Mavra, Perséphone, Symphonies for Wind Instruments.*

Associated Music Publishers, Inc.,—*Jeu de Cartes, Violin Concerto, Danses Concertantes.*

Chappell and Co., Inc.,—*Elégie.*

J. and W. Chester, Ltd.,—*Pulcinella, Les Noces, L'Histoire du Soldat.*

FOREWORD

The literature on Stravinsky is impressive for size and general quality. As the years pass, however, criticism becomes increasingly microscopic in its detail. To restore the long view a fresh arrangement of evidence is from time to time desirable.

Early in 1947 the editors of DANCE INDEX suggested that I make a study of Stravinsky as chief animator in the contemporary ballet revival. This proposal led to a broader undertaking. For Stravinsky, the obvious heir of Delibes and Tchaikovsky, has been also extraordinarily inventive in many departments of the music theatre. If the impetus he has given the dance is a stimulant, his use of the voice is a challenge. There is, moreover, a persistent quality of drama in the whole body of his work, compelling in the very first scores and felt through all of them.

This unique theatre dimension is the subject of our book (as it was, in a more limited way, of DANCE INDEX's 1948 Stravinsky issue). Though widely conceded, Stravinsky's special theatre genius has not before received intensive critical treatment. For over thirty years commentators, with small regard for the function of each work, have tended to emphasize those elements that reveal him solely as an architect of abstract forms. The present seems peculiarly the right moment to arrest that somewhat dehydrating process. During any music season, in almost any great city of the Western world, it is now possible to attend the showing of a Stravinsky ballet or music drama. By this direct and rich experience one discovers how the theatre pervades his work, almost mysteriously determines its life.

From the start it seemed advantageous to make our study a collaborative one. Stravinsky has always been a magnet for artists of the first rank. Fortunately many of his associates—conductors, poets, choreographers, painters—are today in America. So too are composers of several generations influenced in some degree by his music. This volume was built largely out of their knowledge and appreciation.

To all of them thanks are due. But for bringing so complex a project to reality I am most indebted to Marian Eames, co-editor of DANCE INDEX, a contributor whose signature is on no single page but whose taste, judgment and will are imprinted on the whole. In particular it is the pictures she assembled and the research she directed which so handsomely embellish this work.

I wish also to express my gratitude and that of DANCE INDEX to Donald Fuller, young composer and most sensitive critic, for able editorial assistance; to Paul Magriel for the exhaustive bibliography he compiled; to Frani Muser, Joel Lifflander, the music staffs of the New York Public Library and the Library of Congress, and to many experts here and abroad for help greater than can be specified.

Minna Lederman

CONTENTS

CONTENTS

INTRODUCTION

THE THEATRE OF STRAVINSKY

Minna Lederman

It is the theatre through which Stravinsky's music has most profoundly affected our time. For nearly forty years each new ballet by him has been a major event in the life of art. True, his concert scores since the *Octuor* of 1923 have risen in number and deepened in cumulative impact. The contribution of all his works to pure music is of historic proportions. But he remains most spectacularly effective in the theatre. There he is accessible to the larger world.

He belongs to the theatre by birth, breeding and sustained activity. In St. Petersburg, where his father was a basso at the Imperial Opera, he studied with Rimsky-Korsakov and developed in the milieu of Russia's nationalist opera composers. The compelling image of his youth was the splendor of the Maryinsky stage. In early maturity he was drawn into Diaghilev's enterprise and, except for brief interludes, has since spent few years away from the theatre.

His theatre music is, in view of this background, remarkably unorthodox as to form. *Rossignol* is better known as a ballet or symphonic poem than an opera. *Mavra*, the small buffa work, is hardly known at all. *Oedipus* and *Perséphone* are not quite opera, not quite oratorio. The ballet is his favored medium and he uses it in many variations—as choral cantata, abstract dance suite, or vehicle for straight drama. The celebrated *Sacre* is familiar today only as a concert piece.

Stravinsky's theatre genius is more manifest in the qualities of his music than in his treatment of standard forms. Marvelous in their range and invention are his devices for exposing the drama of a situation. But beyond this specific application of theatre instinct, his art has a dramatic excitement in all its musical elements—in its dazzling sonorities, its rhythms, its sharp instrumental oppositions, its shapeliness and precision, its forward movement, and in the undreaming, crystalline intensity of the images evoked. Stravinsky's plastic sense and extraordinary dynamic

Drawing by Picasso

impulse persistently invite the translation of his works to the stage, they account for the theatre survival of such large statuary as *Perséphone* and *Oedipus* and explain the choreographic settings of the *Violin Concerto* and *Danses Concertantes*.

These purely musical qualities are what make Stravinsky a potent force in the theatre. No living serious composer has so many different works in world-wide production. With the exception of Strauss's operas, no contemporary theatre music is performed so often as Stravinsky's ballets. If opera houses were adequately equipped, *Petrouchka*, *Les Noces*, *L'Histoire du Soldat*, perhaps even the new *Orpheus* would find their way into permanent repertory.

Stravinsky's clear destiny in the theatre has been to "musicalize" it. There is nothing remotely casual about the content of his theatre works. What is accidental in their form reflects merely the accident of his changing environment.

Most of his life he has spent away from home. He is a "premature," i.e., before World War I, refugee, uprooted at the beginning of his career. This condition is sometimes held against him as if it had been wholly within his control. He has been reproachfully called *déraciné*, as if the more stable situation of Strauss or Sibelius in itself determined musical virtue.

But his world-wandering is precisely what binds him so closely to our time and makes him its almost perfect symbol. Looking back on the first half of this century we see, within the larger tumult, a great diaspora of intellectuals. Not only Americans and Russians have been expatriates. Joyce and Shaw abandoned Ireland, Picasso and Gris left Spain. The broad scattering movement has finally swept up even the settled artists of Germany and Austria, France and England. In the westward drift, Stravinsky has been a leading carrier of ideas, of universal culture.

Exposed to a new environment he is unfailingly receptive and at the same time resolutely himself. His response and resistance could be charted for every period of residence, no matter how brief (the Swiss years, for instance, even the visits to Italy). But France, his second home, was the laboratory of his most important growth.

Before and after the first World War, Paris with its classic and Catholic revivals was an immense stimulant to Stravinsky. The new humanism, emphasizing man-size proportions in life and art, strengthened his affinity for the western world and his appreciation of its refinements. He adopted anti-Wagnerism, the musical expression of these philosophies, with swift finality. The elaborate exoticism of his Russian predecessors was forever discarded, together with its adjunct of the over-inflated musical apparatus.

But how distant from the French approach was his own rigorous esthetic. The Parisian musicians affirmed "relaxation" as a principle and practiced it with ease and gentle irony. Stravinsky on the other hand adhered to Latin objectivity without sentiment and with a humor that is hard and wiry even when most delicate. His musical "objects" are Platonic ideals realized out of materials that, no matter how fragile, in his hands appear indestructible.

Stravinsky's practical response at any time and in any place is simple and workmanlike. He composes to order with no regret for unfulfilled private projects. If he had returned to Russia after *Rossignol* he might have written a series of nationalistic operas. But he was caught and held in the early migration to France, and Paris from 1910 on offered him a singular opportunity. Assembled here were an almost permanent international audience, a large amount of floating capital, a generous portion of the world's great artists and, until 1929, Diaghilev and his troupe. In these circumstances Paris was fated to experience a renaissance of its special art, the ballet.

Almost effortlessly Stravinsky moved to the very center of this revival. The claim that his scores in themselves justify the Ballet Russe no longer seems extravagant. Distinguished the Diaghilev repertory certainly was. But not till *L'Oiseau de Feu, Petrouchka* and *Le Sacre du Printemps* had appeared in almost yearly succession was the one-act ballet recognized as an important new form in the music theatre. Today Stravinsky can still rouse us by the tension, drama and serious tone with which he invests that structure.

His Paris ballets, so bold in their effect on music, were also brilliant theatre innovations. *L'Oiseau* is the best of the Russo-Oriental fantasies and still the painter's delight; *Petrouchka*, Fokine's masterpiece, is the supreme short-story ballet; *Le Sacre*, Nijinsky's tragic experiment with modernism, remains the century's unforgettable auditory-visual experience; *Les Noces* brought singers, percussion and dancers together in ballet constructivism; *Pulcinella*, which with Picasso and Massine reanimated Italy and the eighteenth century, is the perfect period piece; and finally there is the triumph of neo-classicism, the marriage of Versailles to Athens in Balanchine's *Apollon Musagètes*. Reviewed in this order their very names restore for us two great decades in the life of France.

Still in Stravinsky's French tradition are *Oedipus Rex*, which came at the end of this period, and *Perséphone* in the early 'thirties. They have texts by French poets and in their use of narrators are a tribute to Gallic passion for the speaking voice.

Paris, however, was content to hear the first work only as a grand recitation with music, and to forget *Perséphone* after its premiere. But Vienna (where musicians once found only "schmutzige Musik" in *Petrouchka*) immediately presented *Oedipus* as an opera and Berlin

Drawing by Picasso. 1920

followed shortly with Klemperer's famous production. Though still known to France only as an oratorio, it has since been staged in many German cities. *Perséphone* too has been mounted east of the Rhine and is even in repertory in Prague.

This is not too surprising. Before Hitler, Central Europe was as hospitable to opera innovation as France was to new ballet. One can make an interesting speculation on the effect an extended residence in Germany or Austria might have had upon Stravinsky's production—though as a probability such a residence is almost unthinkable.

It's significant nevertheless that all of Stravinsky's dramatic works, from *Rossignol* on, have been staged more readily elsewhere than in ballet-loving France. America, with no consistent theatre tradition, has presented his entire theatre repertory except for *Perséphone* (so far heard here only in concert form) and *Pulcinella*, though this last has been danced in an abridged, voiceless version.

Drawing by Picasso. 1917

Today, in America, Stravinsky, by one of those fateful accidents which seem always to shape his work (the presence here of a British publisher), is filling a commission for his first full-length opera. We know that the subject has been suggested by Hogarth and the libretto written by the poet, Wysten Auden, that there are to be three acts, four or five soloists, a chorus and an orchestra of more than thirty. Yet with all these clues we still cannot imagine the sight and particularly the sound of it. Stravinsky's past prepares us only for a surprise.

In *The Rake's Progress* he will be engaged, for the first time in his theatre career, with the English language. Now of all the conditions imposed on Stravinsky by exile, those affecting his texts have been the most severe. Away from home, a theatre composer usually has only two

Igor Stravinsky. California, 1947. (Photograph: Henri Cartier-Bresson)

alternatives: he can take his language with him, or he can adopt another. The first is possible when the language is assimilable in the standard musical repertory. Since Russian is difficult, Stravinsky was forced to abandon it in the mid-twenties. For assuming a new language, on the other hand, he appears to have had no temperament or facility, and no inclination to "fake" either.

When he turned to Latin, and later to French, he used them both in a special and quite ruthless fashion. He remains, he has taken pains to tell us, always the musical master of every syllable. Indifferent to the meaning of individual words, he responds to their fragmented sounds. And so in *Oedipus* and *Perséphone*, all traces of theatre intimacy are obliterated. But in the generally monumental projection of both works, this use of sound for sound's sake has a unique and quite towering eloquence.

With its English characters and English text *The Rake* promises us something new and unexpected. But though the accents may be unfamiliar we will hear, beyond a doubt, the unmistakable voice of Stravinsky.

Stravinsky, as the Germans sometimes put it, is the age. This claim, however, he has not staked out himself. He has only set limits to it. He is unconcerned with the "music of the future," has created no system, proclaimed himself no prophet. He is simply a force of utmost immediacy that has pierced our ears, extended their range, re-formed our appetites.

For many, Stravinsky is also an unforgettable face, a bantam elegance, an insistent presence, a name that evokes the painters, poets, dancers, musicians and theatres of the great cities of our time.

Yet he stands apart, in the tradition of the completely self-sufficient artist. His future, like his present, exists entirely in his works. And those works remain alive in the theatre because the theatre is so pervasively alive in them.

REMINISCENCE

PARISIAN MEMOIRS
Le Sacre du Printemps

SOUVENIR OF SWITZERLAND
Les Noces

LE SACRE DU PRINTEMPS

Jean Cocteau

Le Sacre du Printemps was performed . . . in a new hall without patina and too comfortable and too cold for a public accustomed to elbowing emotions in the warmth of red plush and gilt. I do not believe that the *Sacre* would have received a more correct reception in a less pretentious setting; but this luxurious hall seemed at once to symbolize the misunderstanding that set at odds a decadent audience and a work of youthful vigor. An exhausted audience asleep on Louis XVI garlands, Venetian gondolas, downy couches and cushions of an Orientalism for which the Ballets Russes must take the blame. On such a diet, one digests in a hammock, one dozes. The truly new is chased away like a fly; it is a nuisance. . . .

Let us recall the theme of the *Sacre*.

First Tableau: The prehistoric youth of Russia is revelling in the games and dances of Spring. They adore the earth and the Sage who reminds them of the Sacred Rites.

Second Tableau: For Spring to return, these credulous men believe that it is necessary to sacrifice a young girl, the Chosen One among them. She is left alone in the forest; the ancestors come out of the shadows like bears and form the circle. Inspired by them, the Chosen One dances in rhythms marked by long syncopations. When she falls dead, the ancestors approach and, picking her up, lift her toward the skies. . . .

This theme, so simple and free from symbolism, reveals its symbol today. In it, I recognize the prodromes of war. . . .

It might, perhaps, be interesting to point out the part played in this work by each of the collaborators: Stravinsky, composer, Roerich, painter, Nijinsky, choreographer.

Translated by Louise Varèse, from *Le Coq et L'Arlequin* by Jean Cocteau. Editions de la Sirène, Paris. Reprinted by permission of the author's agents.

Picasso and Stravinsky.
Drawing by Cocteau

Musically we were still deep in impressionism.

Painters vied with each other to find new ways of being misty and melting . . . then, suddenly, in the midst of these charming ruins, sprang up the tree Stravinsky.

Everything considered, the *Sacre* is still a work belonging to the *fauve* school, a disciplined *fauve* work. Gauguin and Matisse both acclaimed it. But the backwardness of music compared to painting necessarily prevented the *Sacre* from coinciding with other perturbations of the moment; it furnished, nevertheless, the indispensable dynamite. However, it must not be forgotten that the tenacious collaboration of Stravinsky with the Diaghilev enterprise and all his solicitous care of his wife in Switzerland kept him away from the center. His daring was, therefore, entirely spontaneous. But the result was a work that is, and will remain, a masterpiece; a symphony impregnated with a wild pathos, with earth in the throes of birth, noises of farm and camp, little melodies that come to us out of the depths of the centuries, the panting of cattle, profound convulsions of nature, prehistoric georgics.

Certainly Stravinsky had looked at the canvases of Gauguin, but in transposing them he went beyond the feeble decorative range and created a colossus. At that period I was not in the least up on leftist ratings in art, and thanks to my ignorance I was fully able to enjoy the *Sacre*, sheltered from all the little schisms and narrow formulas that repudiate independent values and too often serve to mask a lack of spontaneity.

Stravinsky rehearsing *Le Sacre du Printemps*. Drawing by Cocteau

Le Sacre du Printemps. Nijinsky-Roerich. Danse des Adolescentes. Paris, 1913

Roerich is a mediocre painter. On the one hand, he costumed and decorated the *Sacre* in a way not too foreign to the work, but on the other, attenuated it by a total lack of bold accentuation.

And last, Vaslav Nijinsky. Let me present a phenomenon. . . . When he goes home, that is to the Palace Hotels in which he always camped, this young Ariel scowls, pores over infolios and willfully plays havoc with the syntax of gesticulation. Badly informed, his modern models are not of the best; he looks to the Salon d'Automne! Tired of the triumph of grace, he rejects it. He systematically searches for the opposite of that which has brought him fame; fleeing old formulas, he imprisons himself in new formulas. But Nijinsky is a moujik, a Rasputin; he possesses the magnetism that rouses crowds and he despises the public (but does not give up trying to please it). Like Stravinsky, he metamorphoses into power all the weakness that has served to fecundate him. Thanks to all those atavisms, that want of culture, that cowardice, that *humanity*, he escaped the German peril, the system, which desiccates a Reinhardt.

Le Sacre du Printemps. Decor by Roerich. Paris, 1913. First Act
(above). Second Act (below)

I heard the *Sacre* a second time without the dances; I asked to see them again. Just as I remembered, impetus and method are nicely balanced in them as in the orchestra. The fault lay in the parallelism of the music and the movements, in their lack of *play*, of counterpoint. Here we had the proof that the same chord often repeated tires the ear less than the frequent repetition of the same gesture tires the eye. The laughter came more from the automaton-like monotony than from the dislocation of the poses, and more from the dislocation of the poses than from the complexity of the sounds.

In the work of the choreographer, one must distinguish two parts. One dead part (Example: the position of the motionless feet simply concerned with contradicting the traditional ballet position with toes turned out), and the living part (Example: the Storm and that dance of the Chosen One, a mad, naive dance, dance of an insect, of a doe fascinated by a boa, of a factory blowing up, in fact, the most overwhelming theatrical spectacle that I can remember).

These different contributions thus formed a whole that was homogeneous and heterogeneous at the same time, and anything that in detail might have appeared defective was volatilized, uprooted by the force of irresistible temperaments.

And so we became acquainted with this historic work in the midst of such a tumult that the dancers could not hear the music.

After this glimpse of what was going to happen on the stage, let us open the little iron door and go into the hall. It is packed. For the experienced eye, all the material needed for a first rate fracas is assembled there; a fashionable audience, tricked out in pearls, aigrettes and ostrich feathers; and side by side with tails and tulle, the sack suits, braids, showy togs of that race of esthetes who acclaim, right or wrong, anything that is new simply because of their grudge against the boxes (their incompetent acclamations more intolerable than the sincere hisses of the latter). And in addition excited musicians, a few sheep of Panurge caught in a dilemma between fashionable opinion and the fame of the Ballets Russes.

One peculiarity of this audience is worth noting: the absence, with two or three exceptions, of any of the young painters and their masters. An absence, I learned much later, due, in some cases, to their complete ignorance of these sumptuous spectacles of Diaghilev who, not yet on their scent, had not invited them—in others, to their social prejudices. There is something to be said for and against this censure of luxury which Picasso professed as a cult. I embrace this cult as an antidote, but it may be that it limits the horizon of certain artists who avoid contact with the rich more through envious resentment than apostolic conviction. The fact remains that Montparnasse knows nothing of *Le Sacre du Printemps*; that *Le Sacre du Printemps* played by the orchestra at the Concerts Monteux suffered from the adverse criticism of the leftist press, and that Picasso heard Stravinsky's music for the first time with me in Rome in 1917. . . .

Let us return to the theatre of the Avenue Montaigne, waiting for the conductor to tap his stand, and for the curtain to rise on one of the noblest events in the annals of art.

The audience played the role it had to play: it immediately rebelled. It laughed, scoffed, whistled, hissed and cat-called, and perhaps might have got tired in the long run if it had not been for the excessive zeal of the esthetes and a few musicians who insulted and even jostled the people in the boxes. The uproar degenerated into a free-for-all. . . .

At two o'clock in the morning, Stravinsky, Nijinsky, Diaghilev and myself piled into a cab and were driven through the Bois de Boulogne. We were silent; the night was cool and clear. The odor of the acacias told us we had reached the first trees. Coming to the lakes, Diaghilev, bundled up in opossum, began mumbling in Russian. I could feel Stravinsky and Nijinsky listening attentively and as the coachman lighted his lantern I saw tears running down the impresario's cheeks. He went on mumbling slowly.

"What is it?" I asked.

"Pushkin."

There was a long silence, then Diaghilev sputtered a short phrase, and the emotion of my two other companions seemed to be so keen I could not resist interrupting to find out why.

"It is difficult to translate," said Stravinsky, "really difficult: too Russian . . . much too Russian. . . . It is something like: 'What do you say to a jaunt to the islands?' Yes, that's it. It is very Russian you see, because at home we go to the islands the way we are going to the Bois de

Boulogne this evening, and it was while we were going to the islands that the idea for *Le Sacre du Printemps* came to us."

It was the first time that the riotous evening had been referred to. We came back at dawn. You can't imagine the gentle nostalgia of these men, and no matter what Diaghilev may have done later, I shall never forget his great tear-stained face as he recited Pushkin that night in the Bois de Boulogne.

My real friendship with Stravinsky dates from that cab. . . .

––––––––

––––

EDITOR'S NOTE: *Le Sacre du Printemps* was introduced to Paris on the evening of May 29, 1913. In the original—the celebrated Nijinsky—version, it was seen only twice more in that city, three times in London, and then withdrawn. During the years that followed, *Le Sacre* moved in triumph through the world's concert halls but was not staged again until Diaghilev revived it in 1920 with a new choreography.

No theatre spectacle of the century has stirred up such a fury of excitement. None today is less known to us in its visual detail.

On the following pages are excerpts from first-hand reports of the Nijinsky and Massine productions. They are reprinted, together with Cocteau's account, in order not only to recall the violent feelings that seized the first audience, but to restore in some degree the actual stage pictures and to illumine the still unresolved controversy they aroused.

The writings of Messrs. Vuillermoz, Rivière and Levinson, and the statement of Mr. Stravinsky have been translated from the French by Mr. Donald Fuller. (For Mr. Stravinsky's further views on *Le Sacre*, see the quotation from his *Autobiography*, pages 147-153.)

AN IRRESISTIBLE FORCE

Emile Vuillermoz

Le Sacre du Printemps demands no analysis. You submit to it with horror or pleasure, according to your temperament. . . . The score should not be too closely examined under pain of vertigo. . . . One surveys this orchestra uneasily, for it is taut enough to snap; all its instruments scale vertiginous heights, its sounds are tragically strangled. . . .

But a secret power brings you back to every performance . . . a kind of barbaric drunkenness seizes you . . . all resistance is useless. At the third hearing you are bound to the music as Mazeppa to the rump of his horse, and forced to gallop, whether you will or not, over mountains and plains. . . .

The strange troglodytes who people the scene soon become your friends. You are fascinated by the three-hundred-year-old woman who presses a faggot to her heart and . . . pounds her feet down on each note of her theme; you stamp briskly as the little men with cheeks on fire now bend toward the soil, now rear up, their fists high, their heads pressed back and down; you watch for the entrance of the flower gatherers whose thin legs cut the rhythm like scissors; you gasp breathlessly at the . . . procession of elders which advances and recedes like a tide on the strand; you see terrified women thrown, as if by centrifugal force, out of the turning, swarming crowd, lashed by the orchestra's whip, snapped up by the instrumental cyclone. And when you reach home you drag from your memory chords of the *Rondes printanières* . . . you even bend your knees lightly in imitation of the Mongolian virgins with their tresses stiffened by bear grease.

And here we come to the fallacy of Nijinsky's exacerbated "cerebralism" . . . What is there cerebral and intellectual in Stravinsky's superhuman force, in the athleticism of his brutal art that continually parries direct hits to the stomach and right hooks to the chin? The music bends the men in rows, passes over the shoulders of the women like a hurricane over a wheat field, throws them to the winds, burns the

From "La Saison Russe au Théâtre des Champs-Elysées," by Emile Vuillermoz, in *La Revue Musicale, S.I.M.*, June 15, 1913.

soles of their feet. Stravinsky's dancers are not so much electrified by these rhythmic discharges, they are electrocuted. . . .

. . . There is nothing more irritating than the laborious practices [Nijinsky] borrowed from eurhythmics that often betray the rhythm. . . . Dalcroze students have a peculiarly "metrical" approach; they are trained to hunt out the strong beats crouching in the melodic bushes. What service can this particular system render to dancers charged with clarifying a modern rhythm? . . .

. . . Yet despite the imperfections of this groping realization—Nijinsky is not the Stravinsky of the dance—*Le Sacre du Printemps* conveyed emotion and beauty. . . . It will remain an unforgettable step in the evolution of a musician whose ways are mysterious and who continues to surprise even those who, since *L'Oiseau de Feu*, have taken him for their guide.

NIJINSKY'S INNOVATION

Jacques Rivière

The newness of [Nijinsky's] *Sacre du Printemps* consisted in his renunciation of dynamism . . . in an attempt to recover the body's natural movements. . . . Movement here is ceaselessly restored, reattached to the body . . . forbidden the singing of its own little romance. . . .

The body in repose has a thousand latent directions, a whole system of lines inclining to the dance. . . . Fokine had made these meet in one single movement, which joined and drained them all; it was to their ensemble he listened. He . . . replaced their divergent multitude with a simple and continuous arabesque. In *Le Sacre du Printemps*, on the contrary, the movement is interrupted and renewed at as many points of departure as the body feels in itself.

Nijinsky also treated the distribution of groups with the same concern for detail, for the singularity of each direction.

From "Le Sacre du Printemps," by Jacques Rivière, in *La Nouvelle Revue Française*, November, 1913.

. . . In Fokine's ballets the groups are always in exact correspond-
ence on each side of the scene, not of course with the ridiculous symmetry of the Opéra, but by a regular distribution of masses, a balance
between them. . . . The balance is not only momentary but is continued
in the dance, no matter through what confusion . . . to the very heart
of its tumult. Each figure is conceived on the formula of an exchange
or of an oscillation; the dancers, taking possession of a gesture, throw
it one to the other, send it back endlessly like a ball. No group makes a
movement except in response to a movement, to the advance, retreat,
flight, or return of its opposite. . . . Thus one's attention wanders away
from the group . . . and one sees only the choreographic motif. . . .
Fokine soon was unable to invent . . . he could only modify his basic
conception. . . . Thus the golden fruits thrown by the tsarinas in *L'Oiseau
de Feu* became the daggers in *Thamar*, the pikes in *Daphnis et Chloé.*
. . . To find a new source he would first have had to renew his sense of
detail, to resume contact with the individual.

This is what Nijinsky understood so well. . . . In all the choreography of the *Sacre* there is a profound asymmetry that is part of the
work's essence. Each group begins by itself; it makes no gesture designed to answer or compensate another, to re-establish the balance; it
is stirred up and set into motion by itself . . . and drags our attention
with it. . . . But composition is not absent, indeed it is most subtly felt
in the encounters, the threats, the minglings, the combats of these strange
battalions. . . . We never for a moment cease to experience the feeling
of unity . . . among these motley inhabitants of the same world. . . .

. . . Aside from its marvelous appropriateness to the subject of *Le
Sacre du Printemps,* this dance style has an obvious advantage over
Fokine's, which is basically unsound for the expression of feeling, con-
veying nothing but a vague joy, all physical yet without a face. In
Fokine's liquid and continuous movement, as in the great arabesques of
the Renaissance painters, the expressive power of the gesture, its secret,
its interior force are . . . diluted. . . . By breaking up this movement, by
leading it back to the simple gesture, Nijinsky restored expression to the
dance. . . .

———

INTERPRETATION BY MASSINE

Igor Stravinsky

I composed *Le Sacre* after *Petrouchka*. . . . Its embryo is a theme that came to me when I had finished *L'Oiseau de Feu*. Since this . . . was conceived in a strong and brutal manner, as a point of departure for further developments I used the very image evoked by the music. Being a Russian, for me this image took form as the epoch of prehistoric Russia. But bear in mind that the idea came from the music and not the music from the idea. I wrote an architectural work, not a story-telling one. It was an error to approach it from the latter point of view instead of from the real meaning of the score.

Massine, who had just completed a new choreographic version of *Le Sacre du Printemps,* understood it in the spirit of its conception. . . . Hearing it in concert performance enlightened Massine and, I must confess, also enlightened me as to the new scenic possibilities of my score.

Massine . . . realized from the first hearing that my composition, far from being descriptive, was an "objective construction." Any musical work grows out of impressions that crystallize in the brain, in the ear, and little by little . . . achieve concrete form in notes and rhythms. . . .

Massine not only grasped the character of the score with an unparalleled subtlety, but invented a new mode of dancing for *Le Sacre du Printemps.*

He does not follow the music note by note, nor even measure by measure. In fact he occasionally battles against the bar line, but he keeps the rhythm exactly. I shall give an example. Here is a four-beat measure, then a five-beat one. Massine might have his dancers move in a rhythm of three times three, which corresponds and makes the exact same total, but underlines the music better than a note-by-note transfer, which was the error of the old choreography. And he keeps up this battle, this slowing down or precipitation, for two or even twenty measures, but he always comes out in accord with any section as a whole.

Since a plan was necessary for the scenic realization, we chose, by

---

From *Comoedia Illustré*, December 11, 1920.

Stravinsky and Massine during their collaboration on the revival of *Le Sacre du Printemps*. Paris, 1920

common consent, my original image, that of a pagan Russia: therefore
we see Russian peasants dancing in the spring, accompanying the rhythms
with their gestures and steps. But I will not place too much stress on this
point: we suppressed every anecdotal or symbolic detail . . . which
would burden or obscure a work of pure musical construction that was
to be accompanied, simultaneously, by the realization of a pure choreographic construction.

There is no plot and no need to look for one. To sum up, *Le Sacre
du Printemps* is a spectacle of pagan Russia, in two parts, that rules out
a subject. The choreography is freely constructed on the music. . . .

THE TWO SACRES

André Levinson

In Roerich's conception . . . the strange face of primitive humanity is
seen through the mask of pagan Russia, contracted by unspeakable
fright before the mystery of nature. The pictures have no subject in
the sense of psychological development . . . nor is the action constructed;
the episodes are simply laid out in a straight line.

The first act . . . evokes the ritual games of an ancient cult. . . .
Flutes and oboes suggest the rustic candor of the first nomad's blow-
pipe, sounds issue from the bassoons as if perforated skulls were beaten
by the agile fingers of a cannibal.

What did Nijinsky do with this music which defies transcription
into plastic terms? In their simplified gymnastics the dancers express the
respective duration and force of the sounds; they bend their knees and
straighten them again, they raise their heels and fall back on them, they
stamp in place, insistently marking the accented notes. . . . An all-pow-
erful constraint dominates them, disjoints their limbs, lies heavy on the
necks of their bent heads. . . .

But when the frenzy of these barbarians . . . degenerates into pure

---

From "Stravinsky et la Danse," by André Levinson, in *La Revue Musicale*, December, 1923.

Le Sacre du Printemps. Nijinsky-Roerich. Paris, 1913. (Drawings on this and the following two pages by Emmanuel Barcet)

eurythmics, when the possessed ones begin to "strike" the notes and to "perform syncopations" . . . it is all over with the earlier sad enchantment, and everything founders in the boredom of academic automatism. . . .

The spectacle comes to life again in the second picture. . . . Young girls dance in a circle, shoulder to shoulder, with all the angelic airs of Byzantine saints. . . . The Chosen One, the victim of the rite, is surrounded, hemmed in by the Elders. . . . Once again I can see Marie Piltz . . . standing in a trance, her knees turned in, her heels out. A sudden convulsion projects her body sideways in space. . . . She writhes and shrivels in an ecstatic seizure. And this primitive hysteria, terribly ludicrous, fascinates and overwhelms the helpless onlooker. . . . Such are the ineffaceable memories of the "catastrophe" of the *Sacre.*

Massine, in a new version of the choreography . . . disavowed—with the composer's agreement apparently—the emotional, magnificently human ground-plot of the work. . . . He simplified and cleared the action by eliminating all historical reminiscence, all pretense to archaeology. Of course the theatre is not a museum. But he filled the gap with a succession of movements without logic, without plastic *raison*

d'être, impoverished in design—exercises devoid of expression. Nijinsky's dancers were tormented by the rhythm, Massine's played awkwardly with it. The final dance still remains the high point of the work, but this vehement yet supple and easy variation, with its *grands jetés en tournant* that spiral like a water-spout—although Mlle Sokolova deserves fame for it—does not compare with the terrible spasms that made such a lamentable thing of Marie Piltz's gracious body, already stiffening at the approach of death.

Nijinsky's *Sacre* was destined to be incomplete, fragmentary. The dancers were like the fingers of a left hand that strike accompanying chords on the piano while the right one fails to state and develop the theme. But flashes of genius had passed through his amorphous creation, whereas Massine's pretentious artificiality remains ineffectual. . . .

THE TRIUMPH OF THE ORCHESTRA

Emile Vuillermoz

The first production [of the *Sacre*] could, with a little difficulty it is true, suggest a novel. Its plastic themes remained vague and general. They were proud and mysterious, they hinted without explaining, they set the imagination in motion and receded after making an adroit intimation. They complemented the score admirably. Now that they are no longer presented to us we realize their qualities to have been greater than the faults that sometimes shocked us.

Massine's version is not in the main different from the original, despite the most ambitious declarations to the contrary. It is, quite simply,

Le Sacre du Printemps. Drawings by Valentine Gross. Paris, 1913

less new and less personal, but no less "anecdotal" than the first. If you call the rounds and the games of Nijinsky "anecdotes" and "symbols," what names will you give to Massine's battle scene in which some of the dancers bind their arms and knock each other down, while their comrades, in symmetrical groups, "play at theatre" by bringing up to

From "La Nouvelle Version du Sacre du Printemps," by Emile Vuillermoz, in *La Revue Musicale*, February, 1921.

their eyes both fists joined in the form of a lorgnette? The anecdote and the symbol can be found everywhere in the new *mise en scène;* there is a rape, a battle, the sacrifice and death of the Chosen One. . . . And the work, which should now be called "Composition architectonique" has happily not ceased to bear the title *Le Sacre du Printemps.* . . .

. . . A ballet master's "rhythmic intentions" after all can matter little amid the formidable hurricane of the music. And the allusions to the "shimmy" that adorn Massine's choreography do not really seem progressive when placed beside Nijinsky's discoveries. Stravinsky's work will always dominate any choreography. . . . You will try in vain to flee from the tyranny of this rhythm. It will bend you under its iron will. . . . All of this "dance of the earth" belongs to the orchestra.

SOUVENIR OF SWITZERLAND—1917

C. F. Ramuz

Stravinsky had moved from the slate-roofed and turreted villa in the suburbs of Morges to the second floor of a fine, early nineteenth, perhaps late eighteenth century house near the outskirts of the town. It is still standing, an ornament to the place. Its enormous, well-laid-out rooms included a grand salon, with three windows, large enough to accommodate even his accumulation of furniture. A half-concealed, wooden stair, shut off by three doors, led to a room he had fitted up as a study in the immense attic. We made a joke of it. Did the doors protect him from interruptions by his intimates—or them from his music? I incline to the latter. Each day the music became more aggressive and noisy, each day less acceptable to the "good connoisseurs," his neighbors, who could conceive of music only as "sweet" or "harmonious" or at least *nuancée* in the sense that word has for members (active, passive or honorary) of our men's choruses, where art consists in the exact distribution of the *ff* and *pp*.

This was the time when the cart of the bride in *Noces* rolled daily onto the scene, rumbling noisily over the pine floor. Each day, seated in her cart in this attic in Morges, she loudly bewailed the fate of her hair, symbol of the loss of her maidenhood. Her vigorous lament came first in Russian; then she would try interminably to express it in French.

It was the time of *Noces* and its orchestration—*ff*, if I am not mistaken, from beginning to end. Intended first for mechanical reproduction, it had to be turned over to four pianos because of the technical difficulties. The pianos did their best to sound like an orchestrion, a device one may call artificial but which I still believe was justified and "authentic." *Noces* was at that time titled *Les Noces Villageoises*, and the original plan was to place in the wings those giant music boxes which have been the style in our villages since the time of Beethoven and which

Translated by Dollie Pierre Chareau, from *Souvenirs sur Igor Stravinsky*, by C. F. Ramuz. Copyright, 1946, Mermod, Switzerland.

we owe to him (a fact too soon forgotten). Wedding guests generally slip in two sous to start things going.

As the bride's cart appeared there would immediately be an outburst of music "appropriate" in the literal, certainly not figurative sense of the word. The neighbors, not knowing what was going on, could well expect to be startled—and so indeed they were. Looking out of the window, one saw a scene of perfect order, neatness, cleanliness, everything suitable to a landscape half town, half rural countryside. . . . A sleepy, tranquil view, where life was well regulated, active but never excessive, faithful to habit, hostile to novelty, that is to say completely rational. Certainly the music was not like that, it seemed to belong to a quite different order when, sweeping through the windows, it invaded the little square flanked by two or three trees like round cabbages where women sat knitting in the shade. For a moment they would lift their heads:

> In the evening my mother braided you with care,
> She combed you with a silver comb,
> She combed you.
> She braided you.
> Ah, poor me, poor me:
> Alas, again, poor me.

The piano would roll on with a cymbal accompaniment whenever the player found a hand free. The women outside would raise their heads, look at each other and probably say something. But no one could hear, the piano made so much noise. It coincided with the carpenter's bandsaw and the engines of the garageman. For kinship or sympathy with it I should not go to the lawyer's office, or the neighboring bourgeois apartments, or the women in the square, or the passers-by with their handsome new straw hats, but to the workshop where suddenly machines began to operate in full force as if in emulation—the crankshafts to move, the fly-wheels to revolve, the transmission belts to glide over the shaft-wheels and the gears to engage; each part of each machine having its own special noise and pace while from the superimposed sounds and the superimposition itself came a new rhythm, the simple, persistent consequence of all these many opposed forces.

Portrait
de RAMUZ
par
J Stravinsky
29 Juin 1917
chez Noverraz
Lausanne

C. F. Ramuz. Drawing by
Stravinsky

This was precisely the progress of the music. Choruses on top of choruses, solos on solos, choruses on solos, solos on choruses. The bride had hardly finished lamenting when the wedding guests intervened, then the father and the mother, then all the other characters at once. The music was swept from end to end by a single current and like a mountain stream it surged on ever more violently because of the obstructions. . . .

The invocation was carried to the end of the first part. In the second we attended the wedding feast. When the backdrop rose we saw an enormous room in a log cabin almost completely filled by a table around which people sat, eating and drinking. An open door in the background revealed a double-bed covered with an enormous comforter. But the participants did not merely eat and drink, they sang—which didn't stop them from eating and drinking. They ate, drank and sang at the same time and together in what seemed like a confusion but was not, because underlying everything, sustaining the entire structure, was the most careful calculation.

The characters leaned on the table, or stood apart, were grouped or single, one minute quiet, then all talking at once, then quiet again. One

Les Noces. Maquette by Gontcharova, showing the four pianos on stage.

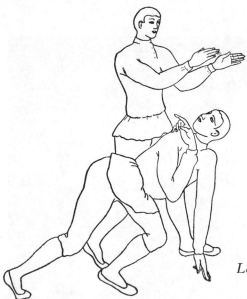

Les Noces. Drawings by Gontcharova

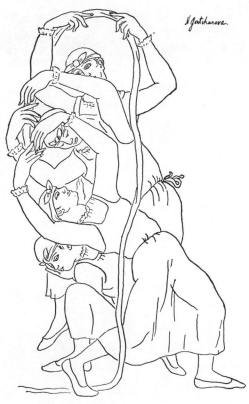

heard an invocation to the Virgin, then to the saints; hope was mixed with regret, the experience of the elders was expressed in proverbs, there was some chaffing and there were many jokes. . . .

At any given moment there were at least four texts (literary and musical), sometimes interrupted and succeeded by others, sometimes mingled, sometimes resolved in a kind of unison. But the climax of disorder always fitted into a most rigorous plan and into a mathematical system all the more stringent because the tonal matter appeared to be free from it. I know it well. I tried to work it out for myself (and it was difficult, even though all I had to do was arrange the syllables), to solve the complications of the measures which required veritable arithmetic computations to arrive at a common denominator. The text, however, could be explicit enough:

> Love your wife,
> Cherish her like your soul,
> Shake her like a plum tree.

Advice of utmost realism shamelessly interrupted the most beautiful passages of peasant eloquence. . . . A man and his wife were selected from among the guests to warm up the wedding bed. Everything still specific as you can see. Even the old drunkard was not missing, never really starting or finishing his song, coming out occasionally with a kind of subterranean rumbling, a hiccup composed of syllables belonging to a word, the words to a line, the line to a sentence, mumbling his story and his opinions to himself as he sat alone in his corner. Like one of our molecatchers with his mug of beer and his beard. . . .

You probably don't like *Noces* much any more, Stravinsky. That's your privilege. My own privilege is to continue to like it. Perhaps you now somewhat regret its impulsiveness, its apparent lack of control—its picturesqueness. Perhaps, having placed yourself, in the course of events, under the sign of Apollo, you reproach yourself today for what your music owed to Dionysius. It is, I repeat, your privilege. But I, who have remained more naturalistic than you—or more a disciple of nature—have the privilege of continuing to admire, in memory, the splendid storm that *Noces* created all one long afternoon, above the little square where the pigeons in their pretty plumage strutted in measured steps. And where the women, who raised their heads, ended by saying, indulgently of course, "It is the Russian gentleman," and did not interfere because many things are permitted foreigners that are forbidden to residents.

To them you were a stranger. May I say that to me you were just the opposite? To me you were the exact counterpart of my country. Not perhaps what it was, but what I should have wished it to be. I believe many things were permitted you there, not because you were a stranger but because, on the contrary, you could never in the slightest degree be a stranger anywhere on earth, never lack a connection with things, with men, with life, could never be apart from beings and from *being*. And this is the greatest of gifts. That is why it is written: to him that hath shall be given.

STUDIES OF THE MUSIC

MUSIC FOR THE BALLET

Arthur Berger

The relation between gesture and tone is always a vital concern with Stravinsky. This is true whether he writes for the theatre or the concert hall. In productions of *L'Histoire du Soldat* and *Les Noces* he prefers to place the instruments on the stage, since "the sight of the gesture and movement of the different parts of the body that produce it (the music) are essential to seizing it in all its breadth." The second of the *Three Pieces for String Quartet* has a jerky figure suggested by the spastic pantomime of a European clown of the time (about 1914). Even nowadays, to illustrate the abruptly truncated rhythms of his *Symphony in Three Movements*, he will hunch his shoulders forward convulsively.

As a composer for the ballet Stravinsky requires no special approach. His symphonic music, so glowing and complete in concert performance, can perfectly serve the theatre. The opposite is also true. The dance scores attack musical problems no less basic than those met by his other works. Even if we confine ourselves to the ballets we can trace his entire growth and resolve the controversial issue of his role as classicist. For although his conversion to classicism is often described as arbitrary and sudden, the ballets show from the start a classical leaning in their control, economy, clarification of instrumental and harmonic texture, and in their rhythmic definiteness.

It is also possible to discover how the demands of the ballet have directed him toward classicism. For Stravinsky seems always to have understood that the effort needed to perceive action, decor and music simultaneously can be greatly lightened by reducing density in the sound. And in still another important way the ballet has been decisive to his classicism, by stimulating the tendency to model musical patterns on bodily motion. In him this tendency takes the place of the romantic preoccupation with emotion. Classicism and romanticism are much abused terms. To define them here would carry us far afield. Let us at least grant, however, that a concern with emotion itself is more in the character of the romantic, while the classicist aims at a just balance of form and feeling.*

Stravinsky has declared that music is "powerless to express anything whatsoever." This seems to rule out a balance between form and feeling in his music, since feeling is denied. But the statement is extreme and was probably made in the heat of polemics as a reaction against the excessive emotionalism of nineteenth century composers. Stravinsky has of course a right to this view—a composer is first of all a man who simply combines tones. But the unconscious, as we know, finds ways to express itself in any individual's life and work without his full awareness. Stravinsky may perhaps even have tapped deeper layers of his being, by clearing from the foreground of his consciousness the more usual preoccupations with feeling.

It is surprising that the emphasis on gesture in his creative procedures should not be more generally considered in viewing this troublesome problem of his esthetic. For movement itself gives body to emotion. Dance movement goes further, it imposes design on gesture through rhythm which is at once an index to elusive attitudes of the spirit and a specific way of converting them into tonal configurations. Stravinsky's so-called denial of feeling, I believe, means simply that he prefers to talk and think of the rapid breathing in a state of excitement, rather than of the excitement itself; or of the slow, heavy gait of a solemn processional, rather than of the solemnity itself. The rapid breathing is a functional symbol of excitement, and so are the tones suggested by it. After all, it is not the psychology of feeling but its manifestations that concern him. Feeling is nonetheless present in his music. In fact, through rhythm in particular, the essence of otherwise ephemeral states may be isolated from the general flow of experience. By his musical rhythm, which is unsurpassed in its ingenuity and force, Stravinsky distils emotional essences that evade others who seek to grasp them in their diffuse state.

Though Stravinsky's native classicism was apparent from the first in this approach to feeling and in other qualities, none of his ballet scores may be properly described as classical until *Apollon Musagètes* of 1927, conceived in the style first revealed by the *Octuor*, a chamber work of

---

* I have discussed this point at some length in "Form Is Feeling" (*Modern Music,* Jan.-Feb., 1945).

1923. Stravinsky's classical tendencies existed in his music together with the post-romanticism of his milieu, until the confidence of maturity led him to transcend and reform that milieu.

Of all the romantic practices that prevailed early in our century the most typical was the indulgence in color, and local color in particular. To the vocabulary of harmonic and instrumental color effects Stravinsky, in works like *Le Sacre du Printemps* (1913),* added those of rhythm. But while his classical sense applied new structural method to the arrangement of color and rhythmic effects, the very fact of their prominence in his procedures established an affinity to the romantics, Wagner and Debussy for example, who used color and rhythm solely for their own sake. In 1923 Stravinsky began to combine the fragmentary effects into those extended, undulating periods and sections of strophic song and dance forms that are one of the marks of eighteenth century music. Nothing was lost of ingenuity and forcefulness, and the structural arrangement of these effects was still maintained. But now the larger, more essential form of his compositions was imposed not simply on the color and rhythmic elements themselves, but, rather, on the subsidiary shapes into which these elements were absorbed.

The type of color that is described as local raises special problems. Such color was, in its origin, a hyper-nationalist device of the romantics. Fearful always of not being themselves, the romantics splashed it on their musical canvas, to evoke environment for autobiographical realism. In ballets like *Petrouchka* (1911) and *Les Noces* (1917) Stravinsky, though he himself had no such aims, adopted the vernacular associated with them. For in his circles, the heritage of the Russian Five (Moussorgsky, Rimsky-Korsakov, Borodin et al.) was something to be devoutly respected—the basis, in fact, of Diaghilev's "modernist" concepts.

But here too Stravinsky reveals a classical attitude that already distinguished him from his predecessors. In his handling of folk material it was the plastic possibility that interested him much more than the evocative power. The folklore in *Les Noces* and *Petrouchka* serves, in fact, as objective matter in exactly the same way that Pergolesi, Tchaikovsky, and Bach do later in *Pulcinella* (1919), *Le Baiser de la Fée* (1927) and

---

* Dates refer to the year in which the music for any given work was completed. For dates of production, see tables on back pages.

the *Violin Concerto* (1931). The creative process makes no class distinction between the exploiting of folk art and serious art. Like the eighteenth century classicists, Stravinsky had little fear of using a cliché, a conventional song or dance. It is the manner of treatment and not the elements employed which reveals the artist as an individual.

The slogan that commonly describes Stravinsky's new idiom of the 'twenties is "neo-classicism." But this implies that he recast, modernized or revived the eighteenth century. Whereas he merely *reinstated* certain principles, as valid now as they ever were, which we associate with that century because it best understood them. The quotation or paraphrase of old music remains as incidental to the basic treatment as the folk music in the earlier works.

It was wholly appropriate that the years just before and after this reinstatement, from 1920 to 1927, should be devoted (with the exception of the opera *Mavra* in 1922) to concert music. For classical method stresses abstract relations. But this concentration had another advantage. It placed Stravinsky beyond the orbit of Diaghilev. After establishing his new idiom, and his independence as well, he could return to the theatre on his own terms. And when, in 1927, the Coolidge Foundation asked him to write in any form he chose, he settled on a ballet, and a classical one at that.

The classical conventions of ballet are not identical with those of music, but their general principles are the same. Emphasis is on line and the organic inter-relation of parts. It is not surprising that, as the years have passed, even Stravinsky's concert works should come to reflect the grace and curve of classical ballet which they now evoke as often as they do the austerity of Bach, his chief source of the 'twenties.

Moreover, the non-theatrical works seem always to have expressed his immediate interest in the theatre. Around the time of *Les Noces*, for instance, there were several small scores of folkish description, based on words gathered from the same popular poetic sources as those for the ballet. Among the by-products of *L'Histoire du Soldat* (1918) there are *Ragtime* and the four-hand pieces. In later years the concert works have become more substantial and numerous. There is almost a decade without a ballet between *Le Baiser* and *Jeu de Cartes* (1935). And though once more, in the 'forties, the dance compositions begin to appear with something like the frequency of his first productive years, his concert music is still in the lead.

Nevertheless, Stravinsky remains for us a theatre composer. If he continues to be so, despite the current predominance of his concert works, it is because, since the *Violin Concerto* of 1931 (which Balanchine later used as the score for *Balustrade*), even these seem to rely for their inspiration on the classical ballet. And, so far as he is concerned, the classical ballet is the theatre.

L'OISEAU DE FEU (1910)

Stravinsky's devotion to classical ballet was already marked in 1910 when Diaghilev invited him to collaborate with Fokine on what was a project of quite another order, *L'Oiseau de Feu*. He accepted, presumably because a Diaghilev commission was no small thing and because his love of tradition was not a slavish academic loyalty.

He had, even then, enough of the classicist's objectivity to assume a task imposed from without—to do a job on order. It is the classicist who conforms, especially in youth, to tendencies taking shape about him, seeking change by gradual steps. From his Franco-Russian background Stravinsky brought to *L'Oiseau* the iridescence of Rimsky-Korsakov and of the impressionists, Debussy and Ravel. But there is, too, in the violent *Danse de Katschei* more than a touch of the neo-primitivism that presently gave so much originality to his style.

Among other features notable in *L'Oiseau* are the economy and orderliness with which Stravinsky organized his musical ideas in a series of concerted pieces. This is in contrast to the romantic *auskomponierte* method, of music unfolding with the fluidity and diffuseness of daily life, allowing no discrete formal divisions and following every detail of the story closely. (Stravinsky was obliged, however, in certain instances, to compromise with Fokine. For example, at the entrance of the Tsarevitch into the garden, the composer wanted to introduce an extended cantilena. But Fokine demanded that when the dancer first shows his head, the melody should be merely suggested, and should lengthen itself out only when he shows his head the second time.)

One of the chief devices of Stravinsky's style during this first decade was to be the ostinato, which we already find in parts of *L'Oiseau*. The device is indicated in Figure 1, by *x*:

Fig. 1. Berceuse (L'Oiseau)

L'Oiseau de Feu. Drawing from *The Sphere*, London, 1912. Adolf Bolm as Ivan Tsarevich

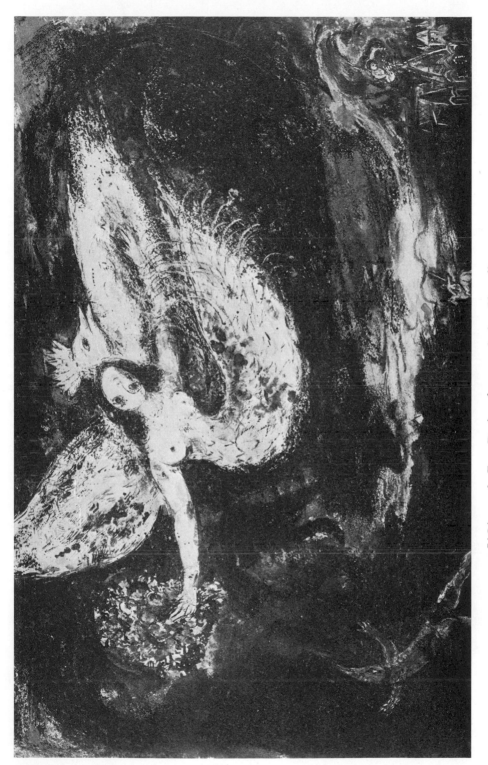

L'Oiseau de Feu. Design for curtain by Chagall. 1945

L'Oiseau de Feu. Cos-
tume design by Chagall.
1945

The ostinato is a persistent, "obstinately" repeated, fragmentary pattern, without any change of pitch in the repetitions. For tribal man it is simply the beating of the drum. It becomes more elaborate when, instead of equal notes, the drum gives us a rhythmic figure. Its function is to induce hypnotic excitement.

But the chief advantage of the ostinato is that it supplies a rhythmic consistency for the dance. As used by Stravinsky, it still has hypnotic effect but serves, above all, to establish a close bond between proceedings in the orchestra pit and on the stage. Now the primitive or folk musician, confronted by a rhythmic or tonal figure, repeats it because he is incapable of doing anything else. Whereas Stravinsky exploits the device in extraordinarily ingenious and unanticipated new ways. The prominence he has given it in serious music is in itself invigorating. Amazing too are his dexterities of montage. And there is nothing primitive about the rational function of the ostinato in providing, to replace romantic vagueness, the precise symmetries and forthrightness of exact repetition.

PETROUCHKA (1911)
LE SACRE DU PRINTEMPS (1913)
LES NOCES (1917)

Such symmetries, as they are found in the three great ballets following next in order, are developed not for their own sake, but to set in relief the unprecedented, bold, rhythmic disproportions of these works. In the *Danse des Adolescentes* (Fig. 2), brusque syncopations (shifted accents) are superimposed on an ostinato as simple as the primitive drum-beat, whose effect is further suggested by the rough percussive quality in the clash of a polytonal chord compounded of two keys. The drum-like pulsations are in groups of four marked automatically by the normal metrical accent of the first of each group. Against these, the extra sharp stresses on the even-numbered beats come as a surprise:

1234;   1234;   1234;   1234;   1234;   1234;   1234;   1234;

Fig. 2.

Strings (with Horns on accents)

Note that the reaffirmation of the normal accent by an extra sharp stress on the first beat of the sixth group is unexpected, too, because by now the deviations have paradoxically established themselves as the norm.

Even where there is no such equal grouping of beats, Stravinsky's music is designed to set asymmetries in relief, where romantic music does not. In romantic music, the device of rubato (either specified or implied) allows retards at the performer's whim. But Stravinsky's beat is metronomic, and when we come upon the indication "rubato" in the charming *Sonata for Two Pianos* (1944), leaving a slight metrical licence to the performers themselves, it is unusual indeed.

The astonishing disparities of meter in the *Danse Sacrale* from *Le Sacre*, under conditions of a precise beat, make their powerful effect without any equivocation. Here are the measure ratios of one segment,

Petrouchka. Fokine with Eglevsky, Nemchinova and Oboukhov. Paris, 1938

taken at random (where the sixteenth-note is the pulsation): 4:5:4:2: 4:2:3:2:3. (Or see the changing meter in the holograph, page 52.)

Not only are Stravinsky's rhythms themselves rigorous, but there is further definiteness in the way they are completely exposed by the clear harmonic and instrumental textures. For the choreographer the advantage is enormous. The romantic and impressionist aim had been to fuse everything into a giant bolus of sonority. Stark symmetries were avoided and asymmetries veiled beneath a nebulous gauze. Such music lends itself as readily to making atmosphere for a movie as to underpinning dance movements. Stravinsky's patterns, however, are so candidly articulated that they serve as exact correlatives of the steps being executed on the stage. And the rhythmic devices so openly presented have a miraculous variety and invention that suggest vast possibilities to the choreographer in his own quest for materials.

This lucid manner of presentation as well as the incisiveness of his

Le Sacre du Printemps. Milloss-Benois. Second Act. Rome, 1941

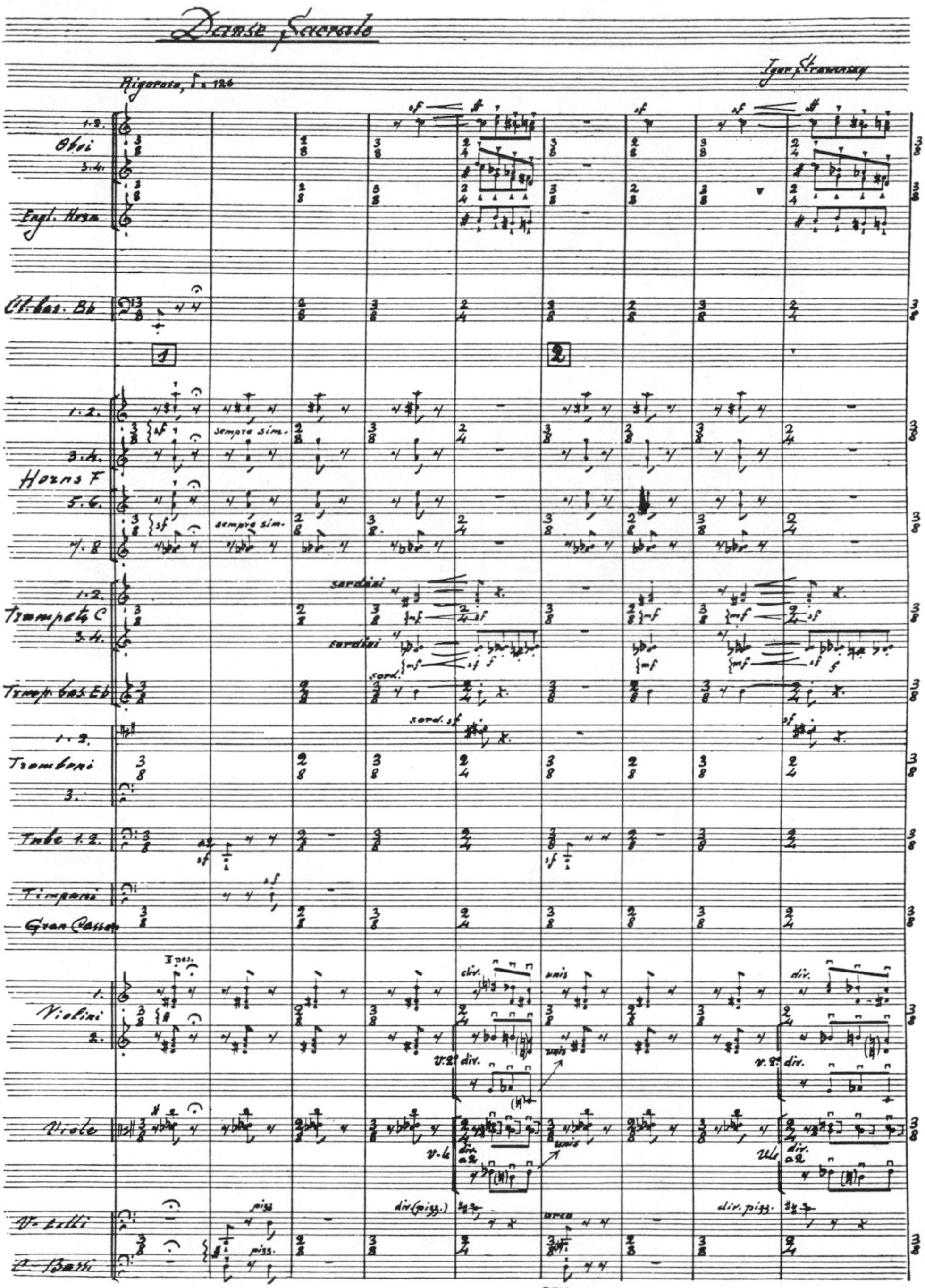

Manuscript page from the score of *Le Sacre du Printemps*.

rhythm were a violent rebuke to the lush vagueness of romantic and impressionist styles. They had the double effect, whether shrewdly contrived or otherwise, of providing novelty to conform with the exigencies of Diaghilev's new ballet forms, and of clearing the air for the final reinstatement of classicism. There was enough dynamite in them to create an explosion in the music world, but the shock was of a kind that results from blasting the ground to build subsequently on firmer foundation—i.e., on the tenets of classical tradition.

Some of this shock was simply a consequence of the barbaric scenario for *Le Sacre*. *Petrouchka*, in many ways as trenchant and prophetic a work, had a quieter story and a tamer choreography, and so its effect was less scandalizing. But if the effect of *Le Sacre* is more unbridled, a greater degree of control was required to keep the subject matter from dragging the form into confusion. (This control, incidentally, is something Stokowski failed to realize, in the racy, turbulent readings with which he introduced *Le Sacre* to this country.) We must distinguish between the strident material and the powerful restraint exerted in its treatment. The treatment is the work's essence—it already prepares us for the confirmed classicist of the 'twenties. Jacques Maritain, as a matter of fact, first regarded *Le Sacre* as a work in the Wagnerian class of music that "debauches" the ear, and only later apologetically recognized that it turns its back on "everything we find distasteful in Wagner," and actually tends towards "strict classical austerity."

As we advance from *Petrouchka* through *Le Sacre* and to *Les Noces* we find less of the iridescence that is so considerable in *L'Oiseau*. The oscillation of horns and, later, strings in *Petrouchka*, to represent the bustle of crowds, is distantly related to the shimmering effect of, say, Wagner's *Forest Murmurs*.

Fig. 3.

But it has quite a new sobriety and even something slightly metallic. With all its ornateness, *Le Rossignol*, begun before *L'Oiseau* and completed after *Le Sacre*, is also at times metallic. The introduction to Part II of *Le Sacre*, at a point where the acid dissonances are momentarily eased, does come precariously close to the caressing measures of Debussy's *Nuages*.

But the effect of the whole differs in very important ways.

No longer is there a constant blending of instruments to make the orchestra sound like the piano with the damper pedal always down. Here the individual instruments and choirs are clearly perceptible. Just as in Picasso, bold, pure colors are violently opposed, to set each other off. Harmonically, too, something like this takes place, but it is difficult to explain without entering into technicalities inappropriate here. Tones are deployed so that their status within separate keys is apparent, whereas romantic chromaticism gives us a constant intermingling.

In *Le Sacre* and *Petrouchka* there are passages that have the transparency of chamber music. But *Les Noces*, scored for four pianos and percussion, is itself chamber music. And while here the harmonic complexities of *Le Sacre* are further expanded, the central tonal core keeps the home community of tones still more conspicuously in evidence. The effort to recapture the eighteenth century concept of tonal center is, as a matter of fact, so insistent that were it not for the rhythmic ingenuities and the gamelan-like sonorities, the work might fall monotonously upon the ear before it is half over. For the note E is a pole to which voices and instruments stubbornly return, and it makes a still more acute dent on the ear because it lies in a piercing vocal range.

The total elimination of gilded instrumental sonorities and harmonic sumptuousness in *Les Noces* is consistent with the informality and ruggedness of its folk character. At the end of *L'Oiseau* the traditional Russian tune that broadens out into a stately close for the union of the prince and his lady still has a nineteenth century symphonic coating that Rimsky-Korsakov might have given it. *Petrouchka* has a cosmopolitan air through the association of Russian folk elements with French street-tunes and the piano cadenzas of the mid-European *Konzertstück* that is satirized in this work. *Le Sacre* clothes folk elements with breathtaking orchestral effects and primitive mysteries.

But in *Les Noces* the almost constant use of voices chanting in authentic folk accents, even shouting and at times screaming, is a guarantee against any intrusion not nakedly indigenous. Unlike *Petrouchka*, which has several quoted tunes (e.g., *Don Juan of the Village* and *Down St. Peter's Road*, used simultaneously at the end of the *Dance of the Nursemaids*), *Les Noces* has only one—a factory song introduced by the husband at the words *"Jusqu'à la ceinture. . . ."* The folk character is, rather, the result of Stravinsky's keen observation of more general demotic practices. The method was already indicated by the *Danse Russe* of *Petrouchka*, in the telescoping of different chords of the same key, suggested by a peasant accordion when one harmony wheezes out while the next one wheezes in. (This device is still present in Stravinsky's vocabulary.)

RENARD (1917)
L'HISTOIRE DU SOLDAT (1918)*
PULCINELLA (1919)

With *Les Noces* Stravinsky exhausted the serious musical possibilities of indigenous Russian material. Since he was interested in the exploitation of the material rather than in its capacity to establish nationalism, it was natural that he should now seek other sources. *Renard* is transitional, glancing back at *Les Noces* and forward to the French elements that were to dominate *L'Histoire du Soldat*. In *Soldat*, the cosmopolitanism of *Petrouchka* is expanded through evocation of the eighteenth century classical suite—a series of short movements, most of them in the nature of popular dances drawn from various national sources. The small forms that make up the classical suite were of a kind that had already become international currency. Thus in *Soldat* we have tango, waltz, ragtime, pasodoble (the model for the *Marche Royale*),

---

* *L'Histoire*, while not a ballet in the strict sense, calls for dancers, actors, a reader and a chamber orchestra.

Renard. Decor by Esteban Francés. New York, 1947

chorales and other marches. A brief allusion to a Russian theme in the motto of the soldier's violin is all that remains of native folk material, but its indigenous character is not stressed.

Since Stravinsky was now Parisian by adoption, it was natural for him to try out the vogue of flip, penny-whistle tunes cultivated by the group later known as *Les Six* (Milhaud, Poulenc, Auric, and the rest). The anti-romantic campaign against *le sérieux à tout prix* (in Milhaud's phrase) was consistent with his own classical leanings.

But the outline of the suite and the anti-romantic propaganda were not quite sufficient to give *Soldat* true classical proportions. Fragmentary motives were more insistent than before. The ostinato had undergone many transformations since *L'Oiseau*, being used not only for accompaniments, but in melodies as well. Expanded through interpolations and other ways of relieving literal repetition, it was by now almost an inevitable device for constructing the thematic line. In this process, to be sure, it did not lose its capacity to discipline the music against wandering. It was still far removed from the sequence—its nearest par-

allel in romantic music—which consists of repeating a figure at higher
and higher pitches and in ever new tonalities that constantly increase
emotional tension. For through all its elaborations the ostinato retained
a harmonic levelness.

The simplest of these elaborations takes the form of ostinato within
ostinato. In *Les Noces* (*Premier Tableau*), a figure of two parts (in
which *y* is an extended form of *x*) is prolonged on its second repetition
by stating *x* twice, and on its next repetition, three times, making the
pattern: *xy; xy; xxy; xxxy*, as in Figure 5a. In *Soldat* (*Petit Concert*)
there is a passage in which the second part, *y*, is a curtailed version of *x*,
making the pattern *xy; xxy* (Figure 5b):

Fig. 5a.

Fig. 5b.

The effect of this procedure is to prolong a single quality in time, so
that the music, possibly through the course of a whole scene, maintains
the same unitary, unchanging character as the decor.

The advantages to certain choreographers, Massine, for instance,
are obvious, for it relieves them of the responsibility of varying their
own line after the dictates of an undulating musical configuration.
Others (Balanchine for example) prefer music that constantly varies its
course while at the same time it is integrated in terms of a higher unity.

However advantageous for choreography, or fascinating in their
own right the ingenuities of juggling melodic fragments might be, one
could not pursue them indefinitely as a substitute for the subtle curve
of sustained, unvivisected melody. It was fortunate that Diaghilev, en-

couraged by the success of the Scarlatti-Tomasini music of Massine's ballet, *Les Femmes de Bonne Humeur* (1917), should at this time suggest to Stravinsky a work based on Pergolesi (*Pulcinella*). Here was a rich store of themes to fill the same function that folk sources had done in *Petrouchka*.

The ostinato now reverts to its position chiefly as a method for accompaniments. Its appositeness to the context of eighteenth century music only confirms what has already been said of this device—it is closer to the classical than to the romantic spirit. Repeated notes and figures abound in the accompaniments of Mozart and Pergolesi. But in classical music such repetitions are constantly interrupted by the larger organic demands (of the harmonic structure, for example). Whereas in Stravinsky, the ostinato, which itself serves in a limited way as a structural device, makes no such concessions. It thus retains only the definiteness of classical texture but not the other attributes of classical form. Let us compare, for example, Stravinsky's accompaniment to *"Se tu m'ami"* with Pergolesi's:

Fig. 6a: Pulcinella.

Fig. 6b: Pergolesi's setting.

Pulcinella. Romanov-Severini. Venice, 1940

The ostinato element is simply F, the highest note of the accompanying chords. In Pergolesi this resolves to E, where the harmonic direction of the melody demands (at the points marked *x*). But in Stravinsky the note remains adamantly unyielding, except at the cadence, where it submits to E.

The way in which the F's mischievously refuse to resolve, exaggerating the repetitiveness that is already there, has almost the air of caricature. *Pulcinella* is, as a matter of fact, like a caricature done with genius and love for the object. It was this love that ultimately led to Stravinsky's classical conversion. But *Pulcinella,* though based on an eighteenth century classical composer, is closer to *Petrouchka* than to *Apollon.* It is the reinstatement of organic principles, rather than the evocation of the past, that provides the real differentia of the later style.

For Stravinsky, homage to Pergolesi was a step in the exploration of these principles before they could be understood and adopted. But for Diaghilev it was like a fashionable indulgence in hoop skirts. He returned promptly enough to his old national-ethnographic interests which he hoped to realize again in Stravinsky's new Russian folk opera, *Mavra.* Instead of hindering Stravinsky's evolution towards classicism, however, *Mavra,* while it superficially satisfied Diaghilev's aims, helped

Stravinsky consolidate his position with respect to the more cosmopolitan facets of his own Russian art. Pushkin, Glinka, and Tchaikovsky, the inspirers of *Mavra*, "had known," as Stravinsky tells us, "how to fuse the most specifically Russian elements with the spiritual riches of the occidental world." Now classical composers, despite the international aspects of their idiom, can usually be identified as citizens of a country. Stravinsky too, while abandoning the narrow and aggressive nationalism of his earlier works, would continue to embrace the broader aspects of his national heritage.

APOLLON MUSAGETES (1927)
LE BAISER DE LA FEE (1927)

Stravinsky did not cut himself off arbitrarily from his native roots, as is claimed. When he was most a classicist, immediately after *Apollon*, he still celebrated the more sober Russian traditions. *Le Baiser* makes use of Tchaikovsky tunes—notably the frivolous *Humoresque* that carries unanticipated force in its transformed state. Not Tchaikovsky the

Le Baiser de la Fée. Ashton-Fedorovitch. Margot Fonteyn, Harold Turner and Pearl Argyle. London, 1935

lachrymose and turbulent spirit, but the suave and elegant ballet composer, is Stravinsky's source. Together with the Gallic grace of Delibes
and the Hellenism of Satie (*Apollon*), and the austerities of Bach
(*Piano Concerto* and *Oedipus Rex*), Tchaikovsky survives today as one
of the chief inspirations of Stravinsky's style. From the synthesis of
these elements he has wrought a new and potent idiom entirely his own.

Although I have anticipated Stravinsky's classicism from the beginning of this discussion, I have little to add concerning its crystallization
in *Apollon*. For romanticism provides autobiographical and programmatic details and idiosyncrasies of style which lend themselves readily
to general description. But it is the whole somewhat indefinable complex of abstract relations that makes any classical work what it is. To
expose the classicism of each ballet score is more than can be accomplished here. It must suffice to say that organic unity triumphs over the
cumulative methods of development by stringing together melodic,
rhythmic and color fragments. Classical devices are no longer indicated
by caricature. They are practiced. Without resort to quotation Stravinsky can now spin out melodic lines that undulate and prolong themselves subtly and adventurously. To illustrate, let me give one example
from the *Pas d'action* in *Apollon:*

FIG. 7.

Moderato (♩=80)

legato

BALUSTRADE (Violin Concerto, 1931)
JEU DE CARTES (1935)

Though analysis of each work is not possible here, we can however
trace the derivation of materials. Since the *Violin Concerto*, Stravinsky's tendency has been to explore a variety of sources for any work,
rather than one. The dialectic play of opposing forces is indeed an
important part of all creation. Classicism, which affirms the fundamental

nature of art, stresses such play and emphasizes the means for achieving unity among varied elements.

In the *Violin Concerto*, after Aria II has recalled to us a Bach arioso, there is a finale that revolves around baroque violin style, gypsy fiddling and a delicate phrase of ballet music. *Jeu de Cartes* gives us more than just a succession of elements. There is an extraordinary irony in the close association of three disparate ideas (Figure 8) between which an unexpected nexus is established: a quotation from Rossini's *Barber of Seville*, a saucy march, and an admonishing figure evoking, whether consciously or otherwise, the attitude of clenched fist at the opening of Beethoven's *Fifth Symphony*. The three repeated notes, common to all, make it possible for them to keep company, recurrently interrupt and follow one another in an unbroken agitato.

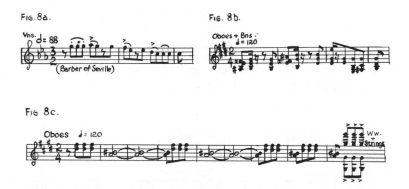

Ballet allusions are copious in both *Jeu de Cartes* and the *Concerto*. I have already mentioned, in passing, the phrase from the second work. This in itself is so strongly evocative that one can readily understand why Balanchine, in 1941, should set *Balustrade* to the *Concerto*:

In *Jeu de Cartes* (Variation 4), one of the ballet allusions is to a specific source, Strauss's *Fledermaus*, a fragment of which is skilfully hidden in a variation of the second movement behind an original ballet phrase sounded out in the foreground by horns:

DANSES CONCERTANTES (1942)
SCENES DE BALLET (1944)

The musical commentary on ballet, which is the substance of the variations in *Jeu de Cartes,* is further spun out the whole length of *Danses Concertantes* (heard first as a concert piece, though it had originally been conceived with Balanchine for the superb theatre work that is by now familiar). *Danses Concertantes* led in turn to *Scènes de Ballet.* All three scrutinize, satirize and distil the essence of the materials of ballet music: the inevitable dominant-tonic cadence that serves as formal punctuation at the close of a dance phrase or variation:

or the flourish of arpeggios introducing a concerted dance number:

The truncated melodic patterns of Figure 13 (shown in combination with a typical cadence like those in Figure 11) are especially characteristic, suggesting an arrested choreographic phrase with arms held at the *posé:*

(The places where the line is left suddenly clipped in mid-air are marked by x, while the cadence is indicated by y.) A similar figure also occurs in the one tender passage of the *Circus Polka* (1942). Many phrases in Stravinsky's recent instrumental works recall such dance passages even in the concert hall, where they become part of the characteristic practice of brusquely interrupting and dismembering the melodic line. As for the more general evocations of flowing ballet style and ballet cadence, they are already to be found as early as the *Octuor*, e.g., Variations B and C.

Scènes de Ballet. Project for decor, by Berman. 1946

Scènes de Ballet. Ashton-Beaurepaire. Margot Fonteyn in foreground. London, 1948

For Stravinsky, each work imposes a unique problem in more than the usual sense. Though dance music is the subject matter of all three, *Jeu de Cartes* embraces it as one of several elements; *Danses Concertantes* dissects the conventions and examines them, as in a laboratory, under a microscope that exposes their most subtle intricacies and fragilities, and *Scènes de Ballet* gives enlarged close-ups of the general fabric, rather than the decorative material, with, as the name implies, direct reference to the stage action and broad strokes that are characteristic of theatre.

In *Scènes*, notably at the close, string tremolos of an amplitude quite new to Stravinsky appear as further development of the fuller symphonic textures we already know from *Jeu de Cartes*. Both works are far indeed from the "pinched" sonorities of the *Violin Concerto*. *Jeu de Cartes* is symphonic in its conception too, in the soaring lines of strings and brass and in its transporting developments, with inspired transformations of the introductory theme (the deliberately stiff theme that comes at the beginning of each *donne* or "deal" to accompany, according to the scenario of Stravinsky's poker game, the dealing of the cards). Stravinsky might just as appropriately have given us this work as a concert piece. It is as if, in creating the scenario himself, he had sought situations favorable to the most typically symphonic results and best musical proportions.

The style introduced in *Jeu de Cartes* and developed within the last decade seems to indicate that a cycle has been completed in Stravinsky's evolution. While covered under the general heading of his "neo-classicism," which we tend to regard as the undeviating principle of his creative effort since the early 'twenties, it still marks a new phase. Here some of the warmer and more impulsive attributes, left by the way during a necessary period of discipline, are reconciled with the recently acquired sober organic principles of structure. Among these attributes are not only the massive symphonic proportions characteristic of music just before he came on the scene, and which he had rejected at the start, but also the strident orchestral and rhythmic outbursts and folkish elements of his earlier style, abandoned in the second decade of his career.

This retrospective note we perceive in the burly peasant-like themes that insinuate themselves into the otherwise classical texture of the

Circus Polka. Balanchine-Bel Geddes. Ringling Bros. Circus. New York, 1942

Sonata for Two Pianos, which could very well bear the rubric *Russe;* in the *Scherzo à la Russe* (1943) (the name is itself symptomatic), and in the colors of *Rossignol* that impose themselves upon the ballerina's first variation in *Scènes de Ballet.* The *Symphony in Three Movements* gives us sweeping themes of almost romantic breadth along with driving passages that recall *Le Sacre.*

But all these opulent colors and large orchestral effects now appear in a different light. There is neither a reversion to the romantic approach nor a resumption of Stravinsky's earlier pursuit of effects for their own sake. For a stable base now exists to which they can be attached without undermining the organic structure or establishing themselves as independent values. Even the ostinato, which once threatened the more subtle and varied formal elements, may now be safely read-mitted, for these have become numerous and secure enough to relegate that device to a subsidiary place within the larger form.

Stravinsky had never quite abandoned the ostinato though his uses of it since 1923 were more restricted. We find it admirable for the drama of *Jeu de Cartes* where it builds up excitement and gives the effect of a chase as we approach the final triumph over the Joker; or in *Perséphone* (1933), at the processional offering of floral tributes, to convey graphically the stately effect of a group walking in a fixed direction. ("*Nous apportons nos offrandes.*") It also figures in those distinctly Stravinskian closes that predict finality through repetition of a conclusive phrase, but that linger on hopefully, looking with calm resignation towards the horizon, as in *Apollon, Perséphone,* or the *Symphonie de Psaumes* (1930).

Stravinsky's latest tendency to consolidate all his findings and re-state them in new terms is but one more evidence of his constantly searching spirit. It was this spirit, alert to the danger of stagnation in material or manner, that led him in turn from Russian folk music, to classical tradition, Tchaikovsky, and the conventions of the ballet. Now his music reflects almost the entire range of his earlier styles. Such inclusiveness would have been unthinkable before. His explorations were in fact designed precisely to exclude, to scrape off the impurities of musical tradition. But today the scaffolding is clean and strong enough to support the accumulation of his own riches.

The *Symphony in Three Movements* has a quite unanticipated opulence which seems to have been exhaustively set forth. We may even expect that a new path is presently to be found. Perhaps the forthcoming ballet *Orpheus* shows the way. The untroubled quality of its opening measures (see the holograph on page 72), the equal quarter-notes of the simple modal contours in the harp, convey to us a certain repose which may explain his present interest in Renaissance music. The score, at first glance, is impressive for the predominantly sparse orchestration that mounts to a climactic tutti only at the death of Orpheus. Through the earlier passionate episodes Stravinsky maintains a restraint that gives a noble frame of distance to the classic myth. His almost

Orpheus. Milloss-Clerici. Venice, 1948

perverse avoidance of the obvious sentiments of tragedy is communicated with masterly cunning. There is indeed a new mellowness appropriate to his maturity. This mellowness, I believe, expresses, in its present growth, the normal curve in the evolution of a towering creative mind.

THE NEW ORPHEUS

Ingolf Dahl

The treatment of the Orpheus legend in Stravinsky's new ballet is extremely simple and compact, the result of collaboration between the composer and the choreographer, George Balanchine.

The music begins with a low subdued piece, of polyphonic character, built around a chorale-like subject. (The use here of so highly organized a fugal pattern as the ricercar, is an indication of the work's formal quality.) This is Orpheus' lament for Eurydice. We see him standing motionless with his back to the audience. Friends and mourners appear and pass, expressing their sympathy.

As the music takes on more rhythmically defined character Orpheus begins his *Air de Danse* which is supported in its middle section by the corps de ballet. This is a spun-out and highly developed variation for the premier danseur. The instruments (violin and flute, with strings accompanying) speak for him in musical syllables of both personal directness and classical restraint. Throughout major parts of this ballet Stravinsky thinks of his music in terms of its *speaking* quality, as if it were giving voice to the inflection of the protagonists and their story. It is not the language of everyday life, but rather a hieratic speech, intoned by the orchestra and by the instruments individually. This minutely controlled music, so expressive through its proportions and shapes, so expressive through its own melodic attitude, is in complete concord with its function: the unhurried, tenderly evocative re-telling of mythological story.

The Angel of Death appears to Orpheus and in a short pantomime leads him downward—Interlude: a fugue on a subject of wide range in measured, slow, legato phrases and an harmonic scheme of the most moving poignancy.

And then the Furies. Fast alla breve tempo in a distinct and even metrical scheme. Excitement through motion and density of texture but

Orpheus. Balanchine-Noguchi. Maria Tallchief and Nicholas Magallanes as Eurydice and Orpheus. New York, 1948

not through dynamics or dynamic contrasts. "The music for the Furies is soft and constantly remains on the soft level, like most of the rest of this ballet," Stravinsky remarks repeatedly.

Orpheus sings to the Underworld (recitative and aria for two oboes and harp, accompanied by the orchestra) in an extended solo. He stops. But the Lost Souls plead with him to continue and he does so in a canonic elaboration of his solo. All this is written in strictly circumscribed musical forms (the music, not being illustrative, never talks in narrative prose but always in a measured, though asymmetrical, poetic diction).

Eurydice is given to Orpheus and a blindfold is placed on his eyes. They dance a pas de deux which is one of the high points of the ballet. Again, it is a non-dynamic climax (as most of this ballet contains non-dynamic music), achieved through melodic, harmonic and textural

Manuscript page from the score of *Orpheus*

means. For the music here is quiet, very quiet. It is polyphonic and introspective, its rising is not one of volume but one of purely musical density. Only towards the end there is a short crescendo (still lyrical) which leads into four beats of silence: during this measured silence Orpheus takes off his blindfold and Eurydice falls to earth, dead. A short coda picks up the restrained melody of the pas de deux and brings the scene to a close.

Interlude: the retrograde form of the first interlude—Orpheus returns to earth.

Then sudden loudness, the first of the entire ballet: the Thracian maenads kill Orpheus and tear him to pieces. Rhythmically highly charged music, *feroce* throughout. The whole orchestra, in hectic thrusts, participates in the violence. These pages, with their pictorially "beating" rhythms, are an apt illustration of Stravinsky's remark (in his *Poetics of Music*) that the acceptance of traditions and conventions does not necessarily proscribe the creation of personal and original music (he uses Verdi's thunderstorm in *Rigoletto* as an example). The chordal lashings of this pas d'action, obviously pictorial as they may seem, are still at the same time very individual Stravinsky, integrated in his own idiom.

Orpheus dies, but his head, severed from his dismembered body, sings on. And now Apollo appears and carries the singing head upward. The music here is of the severest economy. Two solo horns, as if they were the voices of Orpheus and Apollo, intone a two-part fugue (accompanied by the even pulse of low harp notes) which is a paraphrase of the chorale subject with which the ballet opened. Quietly the legend of Orpheus ends.

Never before has Stravinsky so consciously and so consistently applied himself to the creation of a one-levelled monochromatic music. He was aware of the responsibility that such a subjugation to the Apollonian principle would impose on him. But in rejecting the temptations which Dionysian dynamism constantly offers he accomplished a subtle variety of musical means of a much higher order. His insistence on unification produces no more monotony than one finds in the music of Bach or Buxtehude. For the shaping and profiling of melodic phrases, the life of the inner parts and of the harmonies, the vitality of the rhythm, all of these *in balance* supply a truly musical variety that seems inexhaustible.

The music evolves in closed forms: variation, pas d'action, pas de deux, interlude, and so on, the composer seeking a strict musical structure to parallel the action rather than follow it. The unity of this structure forms a counterpoint to the progressive plot development, thereby anchoring but not explaining it.

The fact that at the time of composing *Orpheus* Stravinsky made a close study of Monteverdi and his contemporaries cannot be interpreted to mean that the new ballet is written "in the style of—." While such an occupation at such a time is naturally not a pure coincidence, no transplantation or reworking of actual musical material is involved. Stravinsky works his own abstractions. What connects *Orpheus* with the composers of the early baroque opera is a strong affinity in attitude rather than an affinity in details of means.

Here is Stravinsky's *Orpheus* in the richness of its individual existence. Its introspection invites us to follow, and, in following, to discover the wonders that are worked by fusing inventiveness with control, imagination with restraint, and daring with discipline.

THE DANCE ELEMENT IN STRAVINSKY'S MUSIC

George Balanchine

In Stravinsky's music, the dance element of most force is the pulse. It is steady, insistent yet healthy, always reassuring. You feel it even in the rests. It holds together each of his works and runs through them all. The time in *Le Sacre* changes from measure to measure; in *Oedipus* the rhythms are four-square; in *Apollon* the patterns are uncomplicated, traditional; the *Symphony* of 1945 reviews almost everything he has done before. But in each work his pulse builds up a powerful motor drive so that when the end is reached you know, as with Mozart, the subject has been completely stated, is in fact exhausted.

Stravinsky's strict beat is his sign of authority over time; over his interpreters too. A choreographer should, first of all, place confidence without limit in this control. For Stravinsky's rhythmic invention, possible only above a stable base, will give the greatest stimulus to his own powers.

A choreographer can't invent rhythms, he only reflects them in movement. The body is his medium and, unaided, the body will improvise for a short breath. But the organizing of rhythm on a grand scale is a sustained process. It is a function of the musical mind. Planning rhythm is like planning a house, it needs a structural operation.

As an organizer of rhythms, Stravinsky has been more subtle and various than any single creator in history. And since his rhythms are so clear, so exact, to extemporize with them is improper. There is no place for effects. With Stravinsky, a fermata is always counted out in beats. If he intends a rubato, it will be notated precisely, in unequal measures. (Elsewhere, of course, a good instrumentalist, Milstein, for instance, or a resourceful dancer, can give the feeling of rubato in Stravinsky's music without blurring the beat.)

Stravinsky's invention is fascinating, not just because of his free shifting of bar lengths or accents. He can be very brilliant in this manipulation. But if he had merely followed the line of *Le Sacre* he would have burned out his own interest and ours too.

Stravinsky and Balanchine rehearsing *Orpheus*. New York, 1948. (Photograph: Fenn)

What holds me, now and always, is the vitality in the substance of each measure. Each measure has its complete, almost personal life, it is a living unit. There are no blind spots anywhere. A pause, an interruption, is never empty space between indicated sounds. It is not just nothing. It acts as a carrying agent from the last sound to the next one. Life goes on within each silence.

An interpreter should not fear (unfortunately many do) Stravinsky's calculated, dynamic use of silence. He should give it his trust and, what's more, his undivided attention. In this use of time, in the extreme, never-failing consciousness of it, he will find one of the living secrets of Stravinsky's music.

Dazzling too is the contour of Stravinsky's melodic line, so carefully weighted and balanced, so jewel-sharp in the molding. It now appears to have absorbed and to reflect in wonderful transformation the whole dance idiom of Western music—the waltzes, polkas, gavottes, marches, can-cans, tangos and ragtimes; the inventions of Mozart and Gounod; of Offenbach, Lanner and Strauss; of Delibes and Tchaikovsky.

Even the non-balletic works have clear, compelling descriptions of dance movement. In the *Violin Concerto* (to which I set *Balustrade*) there is the following passage in Aria 11:

Its grave measures, that recall Bach, suggested to me for the pas de trois of the ballet a dance movement long and slow and very liquid.

Below are quotations from the *Elégie*, a beautiful work and a tour de force. With the limited sound values of one viola (it's a great mistake to perform it with more instruments) all the possibilities of a two-voiced fugue are exploited:

In the dance I composed to this score (1945) I tried to reflect the flow and concentrated variety of the music through the interlaced bodies of two dancers rooted to a central spot of the stage. There are also passages like this one from the *Piano Concerto:*

irresistible in the way they bring dance phrases to one's mind.

People sometimes complain that Stravinsky is too deliberately complicated, that he makes himself remote. But may not the fault lie in their own carelessness and laxity? They call his music dry or dissonant. What do they mean? After all, dissonance makes us aware of consonance; we cannot have the cool shadow without light. And we know that to find a wine too dry is merely to express a personal limitation.

Speaking for myself I can only say Stravinsky's music altogether satisfies me. It makes me comfortable. When I listen to a score by him I am moved—I don't like the word inspired—to try to make visible not only the rhythm, melody and harmony, but even the timbres of the instruments. For if I could write music it seems to me this is how I would want it to sound.

And I don't understand either what is meant when Stravinsky's music is called too abstract. This is a vague use of words, as unclear to me as when my ballets are described that way. Does it mean that there

Balustrade. Balanchine-Tchelitchev. Penaiev and Toumanova, center. New York, 1941

is an absence of story, or literary image, or even feeling—just sound and movement in a disembodied state?

No piece of music, no dance can in itself be abstract. You hear a physical sound, humanly organized, performed by people. Or you see moving before you, dancers of flesh and blood, in a living relation to each other. What you hear and see is completely real.

But the after-image that remains with the observer may have for him the quality of an abstraction. Stravinsky's music, through the force of its invention, leaves strong after-images. I myself think of *Apollon* as white music, in places as white-on-white; for instance, this passage from the pas d'action:

Apollon Musagètes. Balanchine-Chaney. Lew Christensen as Apollo. New York, 1937

Apollon Musagètes. Decor by Tchelitchev. Buenos Aires, 1942

For me the whiteness is something positive (it has in itself an essence) and at the same time abstract. Such a quality exerts great power over me when I am creating a dance; it is the music's final communication and fixes the pitch that determines my own invention.

Whether a ballet has a story, like *Le Baiser de la Fée*, or none, like *Danses Concertantes*, the controlling image for me comes from the music. This is different of course from the method of Fokine. Take *Petrouchka*, for instance. You can see that what he has chiefly in mind are the characters of the story. He thinks of a coachman on a Russian street and therefore he recalls the stereotyped folk-movement of beating the chest with the arms, over and over, to keep warm. The music accommodates him by supplying the right beat—here Stravinsky uses folktunes and they serve Fokine very well. But perhaps Rimsky-Korsakov would have done even better! In the death of *Petrouchka*, however, it is doubtful whether Stravinsky's marvelous passage for wind instruments quite accurately represents what is happening on the stage.

Stravinsky's effect on my own work has been always in the direction of control, of simplification and quietness.

Rossignol, in 1925, was a first attempt, an exercise set me by Diaghilev. The problem was to dance a story with a Chinese background, already composed as an opera. But *Apollon* three years later was a collaboration.

Apollon I look back on as the turning point of my life. In its discipline and restraint, in its sustained oneness of tone and feeling the score was a revelation. It seemed to tell me that I could dare not to use everything, that I, too, could eliminate. In *Apollon*, and in all the music that follows, it is impossible to imagine substituting for any single fragment the fragment of any other Stravinsky score. Each piece is unique in itself, nothing is replaceable.

I examined my own work in the light of this lesson. I began to see how I could clarify, by limiting, by reducing what seemed to be multiple possibilities to the one that is inevitable. The ballet, *Pastorale*, which I had set previously to a score by Georges Auric, contained at least ten different types of movement, any one of which would have sustained a separate work.

It was in studying *Apollon* that I came first to understand how

Le Baiser de la Fée. Balanchine-Halicka. New York, 1937

gestures, like tones in music and shades in painting, have certain family relations. As groups they impose their own laws. The more conscious an artist is, the more he comes to understand these laws, and to respond to them. Since this work, I have developed my choreography inside the framework such relations suggest.

Apollon is sometimes criticized for not being "of the theatre." It's true there is no violent plot. (A thread of story runs quietly through it, however.) But the technique is that of classical ballet which is in every way theatrical and it is here used to project sound directly into visible movement.

Le Baiser de la Fée, which I first arranged in 1936, took me a step further in simplifying. It has a freer, easier use of repetition, as in the grand pas classique of the scene in the mill. And again taking my cue from Stravinsky, who in *Le Baiser* makes a specific quotation from Tchaikovsky, I modeled my choreography after the Petipa style.

Danses Concertantes. Balanchine-Berman. Danilova and Danielian

Jeu de Cartes and *Danses Concertantes,* in contrast to these earlier scores, are more playful. They suggest the Italian spirit of the commedia dell'arte. Though not alike in texture, both are rhythmically complex. So in them I have used the bodies of dancers to feel out this volatile quality of the rhythm. Perhaps that is why as ballets they seem to the public more theatrical than *Apollon,* which is rhythmically simple.

Stravinsky, as a collaborator, breaks down every task to essentials. He thinks first, and sometimes last, of time duration—how much is needed for the introduction, the pas de deux, the variations, the coda. To have all the time in the world means nothing to him. "When I know how long a piece must take, then it excites me."

We can't measure yet what Stravinsky has given to the dance or to music. Like Delibes and Tchaikovsky, who elaborated the dance variation and with it composed full-bodied works for the theatre, he too has organized great forms for the use of dancing. But at the same time he constantly draws elements of the dance into our broader musical speech. For dancing he has extended the range of music. To music he brings his own special eloquence of movement continuously felt and most completely expressed.

Nearly forty years ago he began to deliver his amazing works to the theatres of the world. Each of his periods has been a milestone in contemporary art. Today he shows us the humanist values that bind the past to the present. His new scores, grave and deliberate, suggest the discipline and the grandeur of the heroic human body. Stravinsky is himself an Orpheus of the twentieth century.

MUSIC AND WORDS

Robert Craft

Stravinsky's major works are now being performed the world over, his theatre pieces often without dramatic action, his concert scores sometimes decked out with dances. The music, however, has such potency that it withstands all extra-musical change.

His early works are cast in many established theatre forms. Besides *Rossignol* and the ballet spectacles, *L'Oiseau de Feu*, *Petrouchka* and *Le Sacre du Printemps*, his first thirteen years of active production gave us three ballets with voice: *Renard*, *Les Noces* and *Pulcinella*; a theatre piece partly danced, *L'Histoire du Soldat*; and an opera buffa, *Mavra*. Later, in *Oedipus Rex*, *Perséphone* and in the *Symphonie de Psaumes* (a related non-theatre work of choral-instrumental structure) he developed certain forms which by their freshness, individual emphasis and proportion seem peculiarly his own.

Each of these works exists in its special sound world. Stravinsky can be recognized in any one or in all of them. But he has no "representative" score. The singularity of each piece of music is, in fact, the most striking discovery one makes in examining all of it.

Certain predispositions are clear throughout. Besides his intense concern with sonority—his extreme sensibility to "sounds struck, sounds scraped, sounds blown"—there is an almost equal concentration on the problems of time duration. In the large vocal-orchestral works, for the theatre or on religious texts, one also finds typical procedures in dealing with small forms, in combining voices with instruments, in the setting of words and in his devices to achieve unity.

Yet no progressive development can be traced, work by work, in the solution of any problem as such. For instance, the coda-apotheosis of *Noces* is not more fully realized in the later *Apollon*. Certainly the stratification of meters is as masterly in *Renard* as in *Danses Concertantes*. The longer set pieces of *Mavra* are in no way an improvement on the shorter pieces of *Noces*. All the specific requirements of *Noces* are solved completely by its form as are the differing ones of *Mavra* by *its* form. Stravinsky never strikes the match of an idea in one work only to have it flare up in another. Sometimes he even moves by almost dialectic opposites—*Noces* and *Mavra;* the symphonies of 1940 and of 1945; the two-piano works.

But at least two classical principles find consistent expression in his music. Within the limits of each work, order is achieved by both instinct and logic. And each work exhibits a "maturity" of situations and type-forms. T. S. Eliot's special categories to determine the presence of classicism—maturity of manners, thought, style, choice of subject, a community of language, a perspective of oneself in historical time, and an understanding of esoteric cultures in their bearing on the general one— these are all evident in Stravinsky. Living in an age where he could feel no development towards a common style, he was impelled, by an amazing self-awareness, to force his position, to establish his own relation with the maturities of the eighteenth and other centuries.

ROSSIGNOL (1909–1914)

Even the early *Rossignol* shows marked Stravinskian treatment. It is an opera of airs and pieces that are fixed and complete in themselves. Debussy may have affected the first act harmonically but his particular adaptation of the Wagner drama did not influence Stravinsky. Though begun in an environment still responsive to the Franco-Russian operatic style of the late nineteenth century, *Rossignol* reveals Stravinsky's obdurate personal quality. Here we see his special concentration on the breaking up of time, not so striking as in the swirling final section of *Scènes de Ballet,* yet characteristic in its compression into short, tight, dramatic movements. These movements are in a way "set pieces," entirely without flabbiness, calculated and counted out to the ultimate subdivision of the beat. Each is a small unit, tyrannically determined in its melody, harmony and rhythm.

A typical instance is the extraordinary chorus of ghosts in the third act, where three notes are sung over an ostinato of three others, their cycles differently timed, with still another pattern—of major seventh and minor ninth chords—punctuating these ostinati every third quarter (later on every third sixteenth beat).

Fig 1

Chorus of Ghosts: Vois - nous ras-son-blés au - près de - ton che - - vet o

Orch.

Gide must have been thinking of this piece when, stimulated by the sounds of nature and the songs of a native chorus, he cried out in his Congo book, "Oh, if only Stravinsky could hear it!"

Voices and instruments are also treated as a single entity in *Le Roi des Etoiles*, a non-theatre work of 1911, with text by the Russian mystic, Balmont. The integration of chorus and orchestra in Stravinsky's first effort with that combination made a notable impression when the

Matisse and Massine, designer and choreographer for *Le Chant du Rossignol*. 1920

cantata was given its premiere, as late as 1938. This work is also a striking if unfamiliar instance of Stravinsky's fantastically individual sonorities. Though only a dozen pages long and lasting but a few minutes, it uses the huge orchestra of *Le Sacre du Printemps*. The sound, however, even of the orchestra, is altogether unlike that of *Le Sacre*. Indeed this special sound was never to be heard again. Debussy, to whom the almost unknown work is dedicated, was deeply moved by the score, by its flutter-tonguings and slow triplets, its great volume and its tenderness. The reaches of this sonority, he wrote, are of "Plato's eternal spheres," but because of the choral intonation problems, performances should take place on "Sirius or Aldebaran rather than on our modest planet."

RENARD (1916)

In *Renard* we have a completely Stravinskian work. It is a "burlesque in song and dance," a morality play based on the medieval beast epic, in musical form a chamber cantata. It opens with a march and, after the moral of the fable is drawn and the circle is closed, ends with that march. The material is much the same for the fox's two seducings and for the cock's two submissions and de-featherings, and the scenes divide the work in almost equal halves. The set pieces have, moreover, a Paul Klee-like exactness of detail, an inexhaustible invention within a tiny form, and they are linked together by characteristic patterns.

Here also Stravinsky introduced the device he was to find so useful later in *Noces, Pulcinella* and *Perséphone*—the separation of text from theatrical action. This, of course, has its classical parallels and in the modern theatre is by no means peculiar to him. But it does emphasize his tendency to reserve the music as a composite unit, free of encumbrances. Each danced and mimed role of *Renard* is balanced by a sung part in fairly close synchronization.

There is, too, an almost exact fusion of vocal and instrumental lines. To appreciate just what this means one must move forward a few years to *Pulcinella* (1920) where the Italianate accompaniment figures of bel canto dominate the orchestra. By comparison with the voices in *Pulcinella*, those of *Renard* sound orchestral. They are, in fact, placed with and treated like the orchestra; except for slight modifications, the material they sing is the same.

And in *Renard* Stravinsky imposed his first basic time control over a whole piece. By such control the various sections of a work are all strictly related in their tempi to a single metronomic value. For instance, a quarter note in *Renard's* first section assumes the value of an eighth in the second, and of a dotted quarter in the third. Once an original value has been established no new one is ever arbitrary; it is always a simple multiple or denominator. Strung together in this way, the diverse sections make a paradigm of rhythm which enhances the unique character of any work.

Though the rigidity of the system is occasionally relaxed by a pause, a fermata, *Renard* is severely regulated. But *Noces*, which followed, has not even these infrequent fermatas. Its almost mechanical propulsion assures a natural, flowing progression of ideas, no matter how various they may be, and thus becomes an instrument of unification. The *Symphonies d'Instruments à Vent* is perhaps the most important illustration of Stravinsky's power to lock together subjects of antithetical nature by a controlling tempo. This method he applied with utmost consistency for almost a decade, and thereafter, with some modification, as a broad principle.

LES NOCES (1917)

Before estimating the innovations in *Noces*, something must be said about its special character. *Renard* and the Mephistophelian *L'Histoire du Soldat* are both moral fables; *Noces* is the celebration of a rite. It is not only a choral cantata, it is a completely choral work. Except for the final measures, its entire twenty-three minutes of music include but one bar for the orchestra alone. The singing is continuous throughout, until four isolated quarter rests in the last tableau.

Noces is the only work by Stravinsky besides *Le Roi des Etoiles* to treat the chorus as a solidly massed element. Stravinsky's vocal style is expressed here in the delicate balance of solo voices singing in concertante manner against the weight of a chorus *a ripieno*. This instrumental-vocal balance was partly determined by the long period of the work's composition. *Noces* occupied Stravinsky, at intervals, for almost ten years. Much of this time was spent experimenting with orchestral sonorities to find just what sound would "go with" the choral body.

The orchestra of four pianos and seventeen assorted percussion instruments, which he finally chose as an ideal accompaniment, merely repeats
or decorates the vocal lines, giving them emphasis and also weaving a
comment. Sometimes it restates the vocal material in a more simple form.
An example is the scene, kaleidoscopic in its swift movement through
only forty-five bars, that precedes the fourth tableau. The mothers of
bride and groom lament together, while the orchestra reduces to three
insistently repeated notes the essence of their song.

And now we come to a structural treatment that Stravinsky was to
use again and again in his later music, the coda evolved as an apotheosis.
Stravinsky's codas are rarely, and then only partly, made of new material. In general they transform the melodies that have appeared earlier
in the work and absorb the original rhythmic beat into a larger rhythmic
unit. In *Mavra*, as though he were suddenly possessed with the need of
solving the problem by opposite methods, he did add a coda made
all of new material. But *Noces*, though of the same period, has a true
apotheosis.

The concept of the apotheosis in *Apollon* and the *Symphonies d'Instruments à Vent*, the coda in *Baiser de la Fée* and *Jeu de Cartes*, the
cyclical fulfillment in the *Piano Concerto* and *Symphony in C*, the final
chorus in *Oedipus* and *Perséphone*, can be traced to the last pages of
Noces, where that work's essence achieves fullest expression. Without
change of tempo the notes are lengthened. The rite has been celebrated, the groom, alone with his bride, sings to her. What he sings is
a summing up of the dominant melodic idea of the score. Repeating
slowly the significant melodic material of the cantata, the song gradually
recedes. There is also a harmonic synthesis in the percussive chords. Un-

able to settle calmly in B and striving against C♯, the harmonies close with these two notes struck together and a ladder of overtones springs up from the lower B. In a work that is without rests, without pauses, there are suddenly chasms of silence, strictly counted out, between the vibrating chords. The effect is overwhelming.

PULCINELLA (1921)
MAVRA (1922)

Writing *Pulcinella*, Stravinsky fell in love with the eighteenth century. Its classical virtues were incorporated in his style and carried forward into *Mavra*, although the period represented and the type of work are quite different.

Pulcinella is a dance suite of movements alternating with songs. It is not a reproduction of the classical in the sense of Prokofiev's symphony of that name, nor is it a pastiche. No phrase exactly restates any by Pergolesi. But here Stravinsky does make his first use of the traditional gavotte, toccata, variation, duet and minuet. Much has been written about the orchestration of these pieces, too little about their focal place in Stravinsky's output. In them he fused his own individual procedures with Italian classical ones by a common *esprit*. He enriched both his art and his own era by restoring intellectual prestige to bel canto. (It was ballet that determined musical fashion at this time.) He demonstrated, further, a remarkable originality in the use of strict constructions without violating the proportion of the models. With *Pulcinella* Stravinsky removed from his music any taint of folklore provincialism and advanced toward a universal style.

Bel canto led Stravinsky to a full-blown vocal line, compelling him to set it off with a more complex variant of Italianate instrumentation. *Pulcinella* contains arias for each of its three voices and an ensemble that unites them in an extraordinary canonic minuet. These arias are much longer than the tight episodic sections of *Noces* and *Renard* and their treatment is altogether in bel canto style.

Pergolesi was Stravinsky's point of departure for the eighteenth century, the author of the melodies used and the source of the style. How completely Stravinsky was absorbed in the tradition is apparent in the few bars of the duet quoted on the next page:

Fig 3.

Like most of the pieces in *Pulcinella* and the variations in the *Octuor*, this duet at once displays the virtues of the form and mocks, while observing, the time-worn conventions. Only a few notes imitating the old Italian: *She*—I love you, *He*—I love you, are played by the ridiculous combination of trombone and contrabass. The first alteration of the theme of the *Octuor's* slow movement is also a hilarious satire, this time on the very nature of variations with their bewildering spray of notes; and yet it is a real variation.

Pulcinella, though a ballet, uses opera characters evolved out of the commedia dell'arte. Its cast forms a conventional triptych of symbols and individuals. *Mavra* also has such traditional figures—Parasha the heroine, the Hussar hero, the mother and neighbor—all immediately recognizable as standard operatic portraits.

But *Mavra* is a true opera buffa, a Russo-Italian comedy in the 1840 fashion. In subject matter it recalls Gogol. It has a maiden's song, a gypsy air, a stock duet that becomes first a trio, then a quartet, and then breaks down to a trio, duet and solo, forming a pyramid with the quartet as pinnacle. This balance is further emphasized by the framing of the work with an overture and a coda that have no melodic pedigree in the opera itself.

For the first time, Stravinsky employs the traditional opera orchestra. A subtle use of the trumpet in cavatina style to introduce the Hussar's last aria recalls a favorite procedure of the early Verdi. One also thinks of Donizetti, Bellini, Glinka. The orchestra, so different from that of the ensembles of *Noces* and *Renard*, throws the vocal line into relief, now pointing it up, now accenting its various rhythms. It flirts with the voices and yet is sparingly used, except in tutti bars between sung phrases and when accompanying the quartet. This is the complete break away from the vocal-instrumental line of the ballets with voice that precede *Pulcinella*.

Pulcinella. Costume sketches by Picasso. 1920

In *Mavra* Stravinsky introduced a calculated timing pattern to meet the exact span of one's attention for a given situation. While Parasha and the Hussar arrange a rendezvous, eight bars "mark time," in a shift of weight from G major to G minor.

Such a shift also occurs in the later works, notably in *Perséphone* just before Persephone's final speech to Demeter. The effect of this exact pacing is to prepare the ear for new tonalities while it assimilates past material. The whole opening section of the last movement of *Psaumes* minutely "times" the effect of a tierce de Picardie.

Mavra was the last Stravinsky work to use a Russian text. Because he was unable to find French equivalents suitable to the music composed for the original idiomatic and obscure Russian, *Mavra, Noces* and *Renard* have suffered greatly through translation. The Italian of *Pulcinella* and the French of *Perséphone* are, on the other hand, almost as international as the Latin of *Oedipus, Psaumes* and the *Mass*. By using these languages he more nearly satisfied his desire to compose only for "permanent" word sounds.

Stravinsky has always been both individual and consistent in his way of setting texts. Even his early Russian works show the music taking precedence over the word. He uses the syllable for its strength and sound in relation to his own ideas and not in subdued conformity to the strictures of the verse. The result is novel on occasion, but certainly without sacrifice of sense or of larger poetic connotations. In three of the later works he has, however, taken the precaution of adding a spoken part to supplement the sung portions.

OEDIPUS REX (1927)
PERSEPHONE (1934)

Renard, Noces and *Pulcinella* are true ballets for all their use of voices, and *Mavra*, though a short opera, is a real one. But *Oedipus Rex* and *Perséphone* are cast in a new, or perhaps hybrid form.

Oedipus is a Greek tragedy compressed into a fifty-five minute opera-oratorio. All its conditions of performance, all its controls over the theatre are the expression of Stravinsky's drive to make music the dominant element. Action is limited to exits and entrances and though decor is intended it is not essential. A narrator is directed at intervals to condense the plot in the language of the audience he is addressing.

This is an oratorio in the opera house and an operatic invasion of the oratorio society. Its arias and choruses are not quite in the operatic mold; the commenting role of the chorus as constant observer is more reminiscent of Bach's *St. John Passion* than of a Handel oratorio or even the most stylized seventeenth century opera. All its theatre usages—the static staging, motionless singers, "dead" language, and the narrator— center one's attention on the qualities of the music.

Though very different in tone, and even, in some other respects, antithetical, *Oedipus* and *Perséphone* both develop out of Greek tragedy. The chorus in each has the first and last place (Eumolpus also serves as chorus in *Perséphone*), and in *Oedipus* Stravinsky even gives it a Sophoclean importance.

Stravinsky solves the tragedy of *Oedipus* within the set form structure. The "Greekness" is conveyed by the cumulative effect of the arias of other protagonists, and of each chorus, on the music of Oedipus himself. The gradual identification of Oedipus with the chorus is expressed by the progression from extreme dissimilarity to absolute likeness in the music for both. The impact of the unfolding story upon him is registered by an increasing simplicity, by a reversion to the minor thirds which are the genesis of the whole work and which at the same time emphasize the consistent character of the chorus. Compare the first florid aria of Oedipus:

with the orchestral accompaniment to the chorus that introduces him.

Oedipus Rex. Production staged by Schram.
Düsseldorf, 1928

Oedipus Rex. Design by Robert Edmond Jones. New York, 1931

Because the work is stylized, and because it is condensed (Creon, Tiresias, Jocasta, the Shepherd and the Messenger have only one aria each), we are not given a step-by-step transformation of Oedipus. We receive, rather, four or five different views of him. But even at the half-way point his music reflects that of the chorus.

The shifting of weight, by alternating major and minor thirds, first used as a timing device in *Mavra*, occurs here on a tragic scale. The chorus repeats its triplet figures at intervals throughout, but only in reference to Oedipus. The minor thirds sung in the opening and closing measures, and strategically in between, achieve their full importance at the moment of ultimate revelation. Oedipus has come from his first "Ego, Ego" to the humility that has been defined as the complete contempt for ego. Still supported by a minor third his last words move to a close, as the music is cleansed of all ambiguity, in a quietly insistent D major.

Perséphone, separated from *Oedipus* in time and in style by the *Symphonie de Psaumes*, is a melodrama and also an epic of redemption. The contours of *Perséphone*, and its compromise of Greek tragedy by a *deus ex machina* of Christian grace, make it far less Greek than *Oedipus*. Its real subject is not Persephone's fall to the underworld, but her sojourn there and her ascent, in the second and third parts, which resemble the same sections of Dante's poem. An un-Homeric compassion enables Persephone to restore spring to the earth while she must spend half of each year in the underworld.

This difference of character is reflected in the work's sonority. *Perséphone* is the feminine counterpart of *Oedipus*. Female choruses predominate, the narration is by Persephone herself. The timbre is in a very special sense "beautiful" and extremely delicate. Persephone's own words are always accompanied by the sound of flute, harp and solo string quartet, none of which is exploited elsewhere by Stravinsky in quite the same way.

Before the premiere Stravinsky, anticipating an attack on his treatment of language, issued a statement * from which this paragraph is taken:

"I wish to call the public's attention to a word which sums up a whole policy—the word 'syllable'; and further, to the verb 'to syllabize.' Here is my chief concern. In music (which is time and regulated tone, as distinct from the confused tone that exists in nature) there is always the syllable. Between the syllable and the general sense—or the mode permeating the work—there is the word, which canalizes the scattered thought and brings to a head the discursive sense. But the word does not help the musician. On the contrary, it is a cumbersome intermediate. For *Perséphone* I wanted nothing but syllables—beautiful, strong syllables— and an action. This is exactly what Gide has given me. . . ."

Such a declaration of principles obviously invited comment on his achievement. The passages below were cited by critics as examples of violence in the stretching and changing of words:

It is also true that the name Persephone is sung or spoken almost thirty times in the text and each time with a different inflection. Stravinsky gave it three or four syllables according to his own musical purpose. But in the last analysis one does not grant or refuse a composer his prerogative. One simply is or is not sufficiently persuaded by the result.

Perséphone is balanced even in its tonality. A reference to Homer appears in each of its three parts, sung by Eumolpus each time with the same E minor phrase. The work closes in this key, and *Perséphone* may even be said to be in E minor. It also presents a much more subtle illustration of symmetry—the return of the first chorus, near the end, in a wholly simplified version. These passages remarkably demonstrate the

---

* Published, in translation, by the *London Musical Times*, November, 1934.

baroque character of Stravinsky's music; the ornaments are never decorative but structural:

The lengthened note values, the slowed pace, the shifting of major and minor thirds before Persephone's last speech to Demeter have already been cited as a timing device to spin out the sections. In relation to this speech and indeed to the whole work, the final song of Eumolpus serves as a coda. An ostinato of two chords over a sustained bass note accompanies a flute melody which is one of the most beautiful passages in all music.

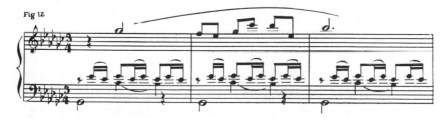

SYMPHONIE DE PSAUMES (1930)
BABEL (1944)
MASS (1948)

The large works with religious texts which are grouped together here have a bearing on the large theatre works with voices. They resemble the latter in their approach to language, in a marked preference for certain wind instruments, in the use of male and children's voices, and also in characteristic ways of striking instrumental-vocal balances.

But there is a sharp distinction, too, between these categories, especially revealing of Stravinsky's instinct for functional form. The basic architecture of his religious works is found nowhere in his theatre music. By this difference, the religious works point up his acute awareness of the conditions that music must meet in the theatre.

Although his theatre music is in its own way pure, he solves the special problems of theatre mood and span of attention by variety in the use of material and strategic punctuation with breaks or rests. (The interpolation of the A♭ minor dance in the second part of *Perséphone* is an instance of how this need for relief is met.) But in his religious works the form is altogether concentrated, exacting and severe.

These three pieces—the part sung, part narrated *Babel*, the five-movement *Mass* and the *Symphonie de Psaumes*—are all constructed with the higher contrapuntal forms which Stravinsky clearly reserves for religious music. No other contemporary has made so sharp a distinction. Hindemith, Berg, Milhaud, for example, use such structures in all their works.

The *Psaumes* and *Babel*, religious pieces for concert use, are as thoroughly contrapuntal as the liturgical *Mass*. Now it is true that *Perséphone* and the earlier *Renard* are also contrapuntal, but only in a general sense. Each Stravinsky work has a balance of horizontal and vertical interests; one hears the chords in separate parts as well as in units. And all the theatre works make use of imitation procedures. But these never are expanded into large contrapuntal forms. When Stravinsky starts a fugue in *Oedipus* he gives us only the exposition, in order to evoke the style and idea of the form; he does not present the form for its own sake. The religious works, however, are made up of just such fully developed structures. *Psaumes* contains a very elaborate double fugue; *Babel's* general shape is that of a passacaglia in which a fugue serves as one of the variations; the *Mass* is all fugues and canons.

Stravinsky's *Mass* belongs in the great Flemish contrapuntal tradition. Though all the masses in the late eighteenth and nineteenth centuries create a contrapuntal illusion, Stravinsky's is contrapuntal in its very conception, close in spirit and form to the *Mass* of the great Dufay. In fact Stravinsky shows a marked resemblance to Dufay, especially in harmonic practices, in his chord spacings, in the cutting of phrases and even in so specific a stylism as the continuous alternation of major and minor thirds. Like Dufay's, Stravinsky's *Mass* is truly Gothic, completely liturgical, more "usable" than the romantic masses that treat the text as a source of dramatic and even operatic inspiration. Stravinsky has adopted the long neglected, impersonal style of pre-Bach composers.

The Latin of *Oedipus* presented him with the advantage of a universal language. *Psaumes* and the *Mass*, also *Babel*, although the last is in English, have, in addition, texts enriched by Biblical and Catholic associations. The text for the *Mass* is perhaps the ideal one for Stravinsky. It is completely conventionalized, the meanings are not new, only their sounds can be treated in a new way. Long before Pérotin the church had authorized an almost infinite stretching of syllables. It is this organum tradition to which Stravinsky has allied himself; it assures him the greatest musical freedom with words.

In direct contrast, the Vulgate verses of the *Psaumes* are dramatic. The prosody conforms in most cases to ordinary stresses, but there are occasional expansions of vowels as in that most extraordinary *um* in the "Dominum" of the last dirge. *Babel* also exhibits Stravinsky's predatory lengthening of vowel sounds in words whose traditional stress comes elsewhere. Thus "imagined" and "another's" are so drawn out that one has a new reaction to them. And the musical setting for both *Babel* and *Psaumes* is full of drama.

The integration of voices with instruments, which we know in Stravinsky's earlier music, reappears in the *Mass*. Here it reminds one

Fig. 13.

of the fourteenth century work of Machaut. There is the recurring discord on the word "Crucifix," a tradition with Machaut like the "bitter nail holes" of the painters up to the time of Mantegna.

Fig. 14.

Short instrumental sections balance the chorus in the *Mass* and prepare for new strophes, as they do in the *Psaumes*. The use of alternating passages of this kind recalls those temple or church antiphonal responses that were originally hurled like blocks from group to group. It is a distinction of Stravinsky's fugues that he interrupts them with brief sections, as in the big fugue of *Psaumes*.

In their sonority, *Oedipus* and *Perséphone* are related to the religious works, but only as concentric spheres are related. For all these later choral pieces Stravinsky has employed certain extremes of range—high horns, high and low oboes—and certain pure instrumental colors (which explains the absence of clarinets in *Psaumes* and the *Mass*). He achieves a new percussion sound by a combination of harp and piano. A general percussive quality is also obtained by having one instrument play legato while another plays the same phrase staccato. Examples are the Creon aria in *Oedipus*, in *Babel* the simultaneous statement of the fugue subject in eighth notes by the horn with repeated staccato sixteenth-notes in the strings, and the first entrance of voices in *Psaumes* that is quoted below:

Fig 15

But though they exploit certain sonorous materials common to the secular pieces, the religious works have an austerity that is absent from

Perséphone and *Oedipus.* The solo voices of the chorus in the *Mass*, used in the fugue "Pleni," and the canonical, modal passages such as the following, have a very special sound.

Fig 16.

WORK IN PROGRESS

After forty years of experience in the theatre, Stravinsky is now preparing his first full-length opera. The libretto W. H. Auden has composed for *The Rake's Progress*, on the Hogarth series, is once more a morality story. It is only natural that the subject, the form and the collaboration should inspire everywhere the most diverse speculations.

In scale the work implies the duration of a conventional opera evening—that is to say a length twice that of anything Stravinsky has written before. Its eighteenth century subject obviously demands dramatis personae that are clear types. As for treatment, we know Stravinsky's partiality to the theatrical concepts of early Gounod and early Verdi, of Bellini, Rossini. But we are aware, too, of his present happy renewal of experience with Mozart's operas. Further, the language of a completely worked-out libretto, by a leading English poet, clearly presents him with more exacting problems than he has known in the past.

Stravinsky is the most unpredictable of creators. About this latest work no definite expectations should be raised. Certainly, like everything he has written before, this too will be truly expressive of his nature and will solve its problems in a new and completely fitting way. Since Stravinsky is now at the height of his powers, it is unnecessary to hope for more.

STRAVINSKY AND THE DRAMA

Nicolas Nabokov

Probably Stravinsky's first real opera will be the one he is writing today, *The Rake's Progress*. True enough, he has already written a number of works for the lyric theatre, of which two are known as operas, *Le Rossignol* (1914) and *Mavra* (1922). But each of these represents only certain specific solutions to the problem. Neither entirely conforms to the traditional canons of opera.

Le Rossignol is, indeed, much more a lyric drama. It reflects the post-impressionist approach to the lyric theatre, of which Ravel's *L'Enfant et les Sortilèges* is a good example. *Le Rossignol's* exquisite exoticism evokes Paris and St. Petersburg of the 1910–1915 period with their love of the orient, that *orient apprivoisé* or *chinoiserie russo-parisienne*, as Max Jacob used to call it. The long passages in parallel fifths of *Le Rossignol*, and the use of the pentatonic scale, are unmistakable fingerprints of that period.

Mavra, on the other hand, is quite a different story. A 1922 take-off on the opera buffa, it is more specifically a charming and amusing exploration and readaptation, in modern musical terminology, of the characteristic features of certain nineteenth century Russian composers. Its prototype is the *romance sentimentale* of Glinka, Dargomijsky and Tchaikovsky, with typically Russo-Italian melismatic twists, invented at the turn of the nineteenth century by the so-called *dilettanti*, Gurilev, Alabiev and Varlamov. *Mavra*, nevertheless, in its clear-cut formal divisions, its buffoonish subject matter and its hero in travesty, is certainly more of a classical opera than is *Le Rossignol*.

Two other works of Stravinsky come much closer to a modern solution of the operatic problem, *Oedipus Rex* and *Perséphone*. The first is called an opera-oratorio, the second a melodrama. Of the two, *Oedipus Rex*, based on eighteenth century opera styles and forms, might be very like an opera, if it were not for its static representation of the drama and its omission of such features as the orchestral overture, interludes and recitatives. On the whole, *Oedipus Rex* is patterned after the Handelian oratorio rather than on operatic form per se. Its resemblance to opera is predetermined by the intimate relation which existed between oratorio and opera at the time of Handel. In the same way *Perséphone*, despite the classical texture of its music, is in some respects like the lyric drama and the pantomime. Its formal structure is without the precise division into arias, duets, trios, and without any of the various kinds of recitative used in classical opera.

Viewing Stravinsky's music for the theatre, one cannot help but feel that he has always been concerned with the problem of opera but, up to the present time, has touched this problem only on the periphery. All his theatre works, even those mentioned above, bear a distinct relation to the tradition, yet none of them approaches operatic form in its totality.

What are the reasons for Stravinsky's reluctance in the past to attack this problem head on? They are manifold and complex. Most obvious is the fact that in the nineteenth century operatic tradition had been deflected toward music drama, and hence toward representational, programmatic and descriptive music. Even such composers as Verdi were not so much interested in the development of new operatic forms and in the musical language, as in achieving adequate support for the dramatic action. In the early Middle Ages music was a handmaiden of the Mass; in the time of Wagner it had become the scullion of a transcendental super-art. Music had no independent existence, no justification except as part of an organic fusion of all "artistic" elements, including the architecture of the theatre, the stage design, the acting (even the acting of the swan and the dragon), the geographic locale, the political ideology, the dramatic action and, of course, poetry.

Unquestionably the demands of the nineteenth century music drama did extensively develop the scope and representational powers of harmonic language, the dynamic powers of the orchestra and the general emotional content of music. Yet, on the other hand, they dealt a death blow to certain traditional concepts of musical form and were particularly harmful to the development of polyphonic techniques.

When the century ended, it seemed as if Wagner's music drama and Debussy's lyric drama had definitely replaced the classical concept of opera. Opera was considered moribund and composers felt that there was no way back to the tradition. But there was also nothing very new that could be done within the limits of the music or lyric drama, after such masterpieces as Wagner's *Tristan* and *The Ring*, Moussorgsky's *Boris Godounov* and Debussy's *Pelléas et Mélisande*. Every new work in either of these directions seemed like a movie serialization of the same old theme, redundant and obtuse like the operas of Rimsky-Korsakov, or hopelessly synthetic and imitative like most of the "operas" of Richard Strauss.

It was clear that the lyric theatre was at an impasse more crucial than the impasse of the *Guerre des Bouffons* of the early eighteenth century, or of Wagner's fight against Italian opera. This situation explains the rise of ballet out of comparative obscurity as a theatrical form. Ballet suddenly became the most useful and successful vehicle for composers of the early twentieth century. It did not impose the tremendous exigencies, in terms of representation, that were necessary for the music drama. Nor did it ask the composer to make a choice between two diametrically opposed points of view—the music drama or the classical opera.

As an independent type of theatre music, ballet had a meagre and sporadic tradition. This gave the modern composer a free, comparatively easy field for experiment and invention. It relieved him of the obligation to follow a poetic text and by its very nature worked against the principle of the mixture of genres. Instead, it directed the composer toward the harmonious fitting together of three arts, each one complete in itself. Furthermore, the dramatic content of ballet from the very beginning had been regarded as a mere pretext for dancing. Hence the musician was not bound by the iron demands of dramatic action. He could approach his ballet libretto as freely as he wished, so long as his music did not obscure the progress of choreographic movement, or so long as the subject did not become completely meaningless and absurd. In short, the road back to opera seemed to lead through the ballet.

Stravinsky, who all his life has been far in advance of his contemporaries, understood this very well. He was the first to realize that ballet

Petrouchka. Nijinsky, 1911

Petrouchka. Nijinska, Kobilev and Schollar. Paris, 1911

Le Rossignol. Design by Benois for the opera. 1914

required a reconsideration of the problems of abstract music, of musical materials, formal constructions and techniques. He discovered very soon that to approach ballet as a new form of program music, or rather to envisage it as a kind of wordless symphonic poem with a simulacrum of choreographic action, leads, musically speaking, to a dead end. Moreover, these approaches contradict the choreographic tradition of classical ballet. Stravinsky also recognized that if ballet were to deviate from its rigid classicism it would become that nebulous form of entertainment we now call modern dancing, which so often has neither canon nor form. Stravinsky saw that the classicism of ballet demanded a new classicism in music.

As early as *Les Noces*, that other achievement of Stravinsky's which touches on the form of opera, and even before, one can detect his serious concern with a new approach to the materials of music, an approach which views them as parts of a sound structure complete in itself, and which was totally forgotten by the theatre composers of the nineteenth century.

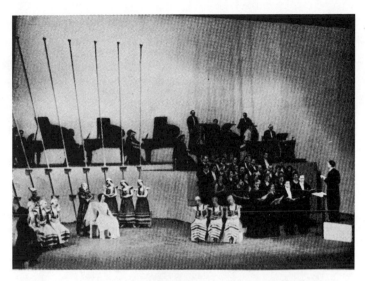

Les Noces. Macke-Otto. Zurich, 1947.

The crystallization of a new style, however, cannot proceed rapidly. There must first be a slow and painstaking reattachment of broken links to older traditions, which demands a careful study of past styles, in this case the styles of the "pre-romantic explosion." What was required was a complete and masterful control of the domain of musical materials, expanded through the nineteenth century's great harmonic evolution and development of musical instruments.

A new classical style, as a prerequisite for a new approach to the problems of opera, was made still more difficult by the incredible debacle that overwhelmed music in the debauch of late romantic individualism, and by the incursion of the music drama and the lyric drama. I also suspect that in the early 'twenties Stravinsky had already perceived the limitations of ballet as a field of exploration. For despite its dramatic looseness ballet did, after all, impose certain theatrical demands upon the composer. It did obligate him to write "danceable" music, to observe certain formal requirements of the choreographic art, and to "harmonize" his music with the general idea of the decor and the choreography. (There are very few choreographers like George Balanchine who know music well enough to make the dance grow out of the music. Music is for most of them a mere "expressive background," or else they

Mavra. Decor by Soudeikine. Philadelphia, 1934

count up beats and measures and base their choreography on the dura-
tive elements of music.)

The field of the lyric theatre was no more suitable for Stravinsky's
particular kind of exploration. As I suggested before, the road to classical opera was blocked by the dusty trophies of the music drama. And
more, classical opera at its best is the summit of all musical forms. It requires a ripeness of style, a well-blended and well-aged stylistic perfection, none of which were in existence at this point of Stravinsky's career.
Without such support the opera composer becomes the slave of the
poetic idea or the dramatic situation.

This explains Stravinsky's intense interest in pure or abstract forms.
It was in fact inevitable. The new classical style had to evolve out of
instrumental music. When Stravinsky again turned to the ballet and
drama, during the 'twenties and 'thirties, these forms became problems
of pure music. He did not of course fail to consider carefully and to
fulfill in his music the dramatic or poetic implications of his ballets or
"semi-operatic" oratorios. On the contrary, this dramatic evocation is
poignant and exhaustive. His main concern, nevertheless, is primarily
that of a composer writing a piece of music, valid and complete on its
own musical terms.

In his exploration of the outer reaches of opera, Stravinsky has
made a number of discoveries: new methods, devices and techniques. Or
rather, he has successfully developed old ones in new and unexpected
directions. He was able to do so chiefly *because* he was approaching
opera—or ballet, for that matter—as a problem of musical construction.
For example his orchestral technique, which is based entirely on the individuality of each instrument, makes his orchestra an extraordinary
precision instrument for measuring and describing a given dramatic situation. Let me explain more fully what I mean by giving an example
from one of his recent works, *Orpheus*, which, I should add, though
entitled a ballet, seems to me primarily a drama without voices.

The epilogue of *Orpheus* is a canonic fugue between two horns—its
theme an inversion of one that appears at the beginning—over a cantus
firmus sung in unison by one trumpet and one violin, which together
produce a characteristically medieval sound, the sound of a *vielle*. One
harp plucks an accompaniment to this three-part medieval-sounding

polyphony. At regular intervals the fugue is interrupted (or as Stravinsky explained to me, "cut off with a pair of scissors") by a short two-bar phrase, a harp solo that sounds like an accompaniment to a non-existent melody.

The dramatic situation is as follows: Orpheus has just been torn to shreds by the Thracian women or, as Stravinsky's music and Balanchine's choreography suggest, a bloodless, inevitable and dispassionate operation has been performed on the body of hopeless Orpheus. Orpheus is no more; Orpheus is dead. The world is without song, mute and desolate. Apollo's hymn to the memory of the dead hero, and his attempt to play the lyre, enhance the melancholy realization of Orpheus' death. In the hands of Apollo the lyre sounds like the forlorn accompaniment to a song that is lost forever. The translation of a simple dramatic situation into an equally simple musical form is executed with incredible lucidity and with the microscope precision of a laboratory scientist.

Stravinsky's approach is always the same; he uses a remarkable economy of means, which is determined by an infallible sense of proportion, time and form.

The ingenious instrumental combinations of this epilogue, and the slow and majestic flow of its polyphonic lines, bring out the meaning of the dramatic situation. The very choice of instruments to sing those expressive, sad melodies is significant: two French horns and one trumpet, purposely not strings, to suggest the lyre, the instrument of Orpheus' choice.

The melodic lines could have been distributed to violas and cellos, for example. And in a sense the character and general outlines of these melodies do suggest the bowing of strings. Yet had Stravinsky chosen such instruments, he would never have given to these somber themes the tense quality of anguish that is evoked by two bleating horns and one lonely trumpet. No other instruments of our modern orchestra can equal the brasses—horns particularly—in this special evocative power. When they sing a sad, lyric melody in their upper register they sound strangled, precarious, tragic.

Here Stravinsky not only exhibits his uncanny sense of the individuality, or better, the personality of musical instruments, but he also discovers an extremely effective and *musical* way of stating a dramatic situation. The drama is reinforced by extending the technical possibilities of the instruments.

It is important to point out that Stravinsky has always explored these possibilities to the limits of individual register, velocity, or degree of potential intricacy in the rhythmic design. He has often exploited these instrumental limits with great effectiveness in describing a dramatic situation—in the scene, *Chez Petrouchka* (the clarinet); in certain parts of *Orpheus* and *Apollon;* in the finale of *Les Noces,* and in many other instances. Each time the particular character of an instrument used in its most precarious registers, or in an unusual or unexpected way, becomes a kind of agent or carrier.

Reviewing Stravinsky's many works for the theatre, one is struck by a recurrent choice of subjects, or rather by the recurrence of the same central idea. Stated in terms of *Petrouchka,* this central idea is two-fold: one, man is a toy in the hands of impenetrable, cruel and amoral forces; and two, life is a kind of mechanism of destiny wherein free will plays no part.

It is interesting to note how often in his theatre work Stravinsky represents his dramatis personae either as puppets or animals, without free will. In *Les Noces,* for example, from beginning to end of this remarkable work, one sees the ritual of marriage described as a kind of mechanical succession of events that lead, with cruel inevitability, to the conjugal sacrifice of the bride to the groom. *Jeu de Cartes* is another instance where the mechanical character of life is stressed, symbolized here by four poker hands. And finally, in the tragedy of *Oedipus Rex,* that classic symbol of man in the grip of immutable destiny, the king is presented by Stravinsky as the victim of a *machine infernale.* This Manichean *Weltanschauung* pervades most of Stravinsky's work for the theatre. In different variations, it appears in *L'Histoire du Soldat, Renard* and *Le Rossignol.*

But this approach extends beyond his choice of subjects. It controls the very treatment of musical materials, to which he so cleverly applies this mechanization. He does it by means of the most scrupulous measurements of timing, expressive lines, dynamic changes and interval relations. He reconstructs in a dramatic work the precise mechanics of a

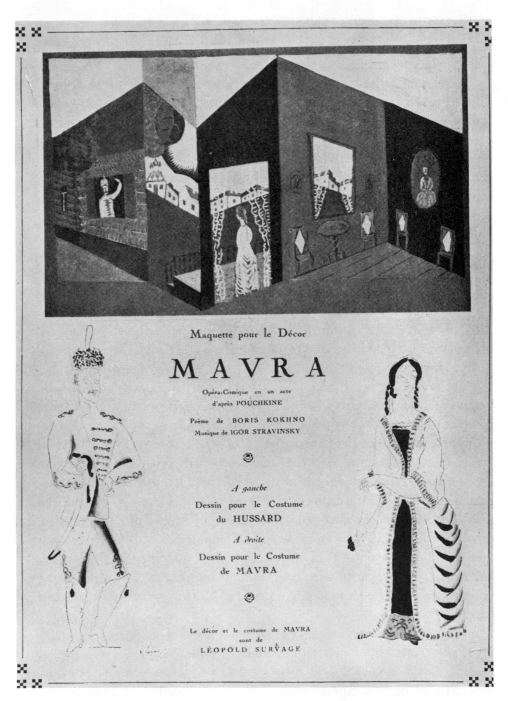

Maquette pour le Décor

MAVRA

Opéra-Comique en un acte
d'après POUCHKINE

Poème de BORIS KOKHNO
Musique de IGOR STRAVINSKY

A gauche

Dessin pour le Costume
du HUSSARD

A droite

Dessin pour le Costume
de MAVRA

Le décor et le costume de MAVRA
sont de
LÉOPOLD SURVAGE

Page from a Diaghilev souvenir program. May–June, 1922

Petrouchka. Choreography by Gsovsky. Jahnke and Trofimova as Petrouchka and the Ballerina. Berlin, 1947

Perséphone. Macke-Otto. Zurich, 1947

dramatic situation. He leaves the listener no room for an interpretative variation or a vague phantasy.

As he often says, his work is as precise, as complete and exact as a "police report" or "minutes of the proceedings." It seems to me that these specific qualities of his music and his general *Weltanschauung* enhance his sense of drama. They will make him, I believe, the precursor of a new era in the evolution of operatic form. Having developed a style of his own, brilliant, homogeneous and immensely resourceful, Stravinsky is now coming to grips with the greatest of all forms of Western music, the classical opera.

APPRECIATION

STRAVINSKY'S GIFT TO THE WEST

Ernest Ansermet

It was because the melody and harmony were so fresh that we found Russian music irresistible. This freshness was no matter of chance. Musicians of the West had established the foundation of their whole tonal concept, both melodic and harmonic, upon the relation of a tone to its dominant. Striving for an expressive system that should be rational, little by little they reduced all steps and figures to the affirmation of this relationship. For this system Rameau evolved his theory. Admirable as it was, it represented only a certain condensation of all the resources of the art. It remained for music in our time to open up new possibilities.

The Russians, however, had no part in that tradition. Although their music recognized the essential character of this relationship, it did not make the same use of it. At the time that Stravinsky started to compose, Russian music was a hundred years old. But it had begun to show a certain weakening of force. This was one reason impelling Stravinsky to leave his fatherland. He felt more free to fulfill his destiny in the climate of Debussy and Ravel than in a St. Petersburg haunted by Wagner. But this much is clear. Though he chose to live, from then on, among foreign musicians, it was to create in a fashion unlike theirs.

Beginning with the theme of *Petrouchka* we find him oriented toward polytonality. This term is generally understood only in the light of classic theory. For Stravinsky, however, it came to signify a new and broader concept of tonality, leading him along paths where he could remain tonal beyond the conventional meaning of that word. Here is an example, from the *Symphonies for Wind Instruments*, that is simple and succinct:

It would be absurd to see in the second measure of this motif a chord made up of B♭–G–B♮. The B♭ refers to the F, the B♮ to the D. The three measures form but one unit in musical time—a melodic movement around one note, the D, which leans, on the one hand, toward the G and, in the other direction of the sound-space, toward the F-B♭. In other words, Stravinsky imposes upon a duration of time the order of simultaneity, and this permits him to bring together, in a single time-space, multiple harmonic relations that yet remain distinct.

It is a familiar illusion of memory to confuse the experience of a melody with its final effect. When we hear the opening air on the flute in *L'Après-midi d'un Faune* we perceive it as a whole within our immediate horizon. It is fundamental to the experience of music that we find ourselves in the presence of a transcendent object (the melody) which extends through time, exactly as we confront a world extended in space. On the other hand, we are too inclined to associate harmonic relations with simultaneity. Simultaneity cannot be reduced to an instant, which is only, as Sartre would say, an interval of nothingness. It implies duration—otherwise the appoggiatura and the retard would never have been possible.

Stravinsky's prime achievement, and his alone, is to have realized that in music the present is extended. By organizing his harmonic relations not only in strict simultaneity but in this extension during which we perceive a motif, a phrase, a whole musical period, he has returned to the very sources of our art, giving to himself a new impetus of infinite possibilities and, at the same time, to us a sharper, richer and more vital consciousness of the sound-space where musical forms are deployed—the world indeed in which musicians have their being.

Understanding this, we can estimate in its true proportions the character of Stravinsky's creative act. At a time when others were trying to find their way by theoretical speculation, he held to the concrete. His innovations proceed from a fresh and direct renewal of his musical sense, a continually deepening awareness of the sentient world. They open up for us a new musical realism. This realism, which we find in his rhythms or his distribution of timbres, penetrates all his production. It explains that extraordinarily sure workmanship which recalls the old masters. In this respect it is wrong to differentiate between his music for concert performance—in general that of his later period—and his celebrated ballets. There is just as great mastery, there are just as many vitamins, if I may say so, in an apparently insignificant score like *Norwegian Moods*, as in the works that won immediate public acceptance. Clearly it required a singular inventive force to bring to music of an autonomous character—that is without any extra-musical subject—an art like Stravinsky's which seemed to be dedicated to imagery.

His music obviously implies a whole esthetic, a fundamental attitude on the part of the artist toward his art. Like any esthetic position this might itself be the subject of discussion. But such a discussion could never in the end diminish the importance of Stravinsky's creative achievement. This has the force of a fact. It has brought to music an enrichment that none can dispute.

Translated by Frani Muser

INFLUENCE, PROBLEM, TONE

Aaron Copland

If we can gauge the vitality of a composer's work by the extent of his influence, then Stravinsky's record is an enviable one. For more than thirty years his music has exercised a continuing hold which is without parallel since Wagner's day. In the twentieth century, only Debussy cast a comparable spell, and that was of a limited nature and of a single style. It is one of the curiosities of contemporary musical history that Stravinsky has been able to influence two succeeding generations in ways diametrically opposed.

Because of Stravinsky, the period 1917–1927 was the decade of the displaced accent and the polytonal chord. Few escaped the impact of his personality. The frenetic dynamism and harmonic daring of *Le Sacre* were reflected in other ballets, Prokofiev's *Age of Steel*, Chavez' *H.P.* (Horse Power), Carpenter's *Skyscrapers*. Antheil's *Ballet Mécanique* was a reductio ad absurdum of Stravinsky's emphasis on furious rhythms and pitiless dissonances.

Then suddenly, with almost no warning, Stravinsky executed an about-face that startled and confused everyone. Everyone but the composers, that is. For despite repeated critical accusations of sterility and an apathetic public response, many composers rallied to the new cause of neo-classicism. Once more Stravinsky had called the tune.

In America one can trace a straight line from Roger Sessions' *First Symphony* (1927) to Harold Shapero's *Serenade for String Orchestra* (1946). Among our younger generation it is easy to discover a Stravinsky school: Shapero, Haieff, Berger, Lessard, Foss, Fine.

Looking ahead one can foresee still a third type of Stravinsky influence, based upon the formal-structural peculiarities of works like *Scènes de Ballet, Ebony Concerto* and especially the recent *Symphony in Three Movements*. The organization of musical materials in the first movement of the *Symphony* opens new paths into the little explored region of musical coherence.

Isn't it surprising that, at the age of sixty-five, Stravinsky is still writing problem music? All the other composers over fifty—the famous ones, I mean—are turning out more or less what is expected of them. It seems a long time since we got a jolt from Hindemith. Schönberg's latest is problematical certainly, but in the same way it has been for the past thirty years. Milhaud, Honegger, Prokofiev are all sticking close to form. Only Stravinsky manages to mix his elements, including even the familiar ones, in such a way that no one can predict just where he will be taking us next.

But perhaps the most impressive point of all is that over and beyond the questions of problem or influence there remains in Stravinsky's music an irreducible core that defies imitation. The essence of the man— his special "tone," his very personal brand of seriousness, the non-academic texture of his music—in short, the sum total of his extraordinary individuality, has never to my knowledge been adequately described, let alone imitated. Despite the widespread influence of his music, Stravinsky as a composer remains a singularly remote and removed figure, a composer whose passport to the future needs no signature other than his own.

———

THE ARTIST AND THE MAN

Alexei Haieff

Stravinsky is a composer who lives by his music as a shoemaker does by his cobbling or a banker by his strategy with money. Our generation has adapted itself to the idea that a composer is a special person in a special situation. But to Stravinsky music is, as it should be to anyone, an honest occupation. He faces life as a man who, without any inhibitions, simply makes music. With him to live is to compose; to compose is to live.

When he talks of "my career" it is not with the usual professional emphasis. His work and his life together make him what he is. He belongs to the line of great men whose perseverance in living as artists completely justifies their right to the title.

Stravinsky cannot imagine separating the task of composing from that of providing for the needs, say, of his cat. He will provide nourishment for his cat by composing. For his hobbies, flowers, books, wines, he "arranges" time around his composing. Other men arrange time to compose. For them art is sacred, which no doubt it is. But to keep it sacred, they must separate the pursuit of livelihood from the pursuit of art. Thus the livelihood becomes life and art becomes a hobby.

If he were asked to write an "Overture to the Moon," I feel sure Stravinsky would take the commission. He would execute it quite honestly. The finished work would represent exactly what he feels and what he can accomplish at this particular moment. He would not try to guess what those who commissioned him might have in mind. Certainly he would not want to imagine what his audience expects to hear about the moon. He does not uplift the public by writing down to it. His approach is simple. As a human being he will be humble toward his work, as an artist he will do his best—and that is all.

To many, the results of Stravinsky's continuous evolution as a composer may be disappointing. The miracle they themselves have imagined is not realized—he gives them no plushy wooing of the moon, and the universe does not stand still. Ever since *Le Sacre*, the mass public has been jolted by his failure to provide for its satisfaction the same thrill, spectacle and excitement. The reality of what he does produce is always unforeseen. Many find the music too "purely musical."

And yet this music always works, by its force, its solidity as music. Most especially as music for the theatre, it renews our joy in the theatre.

The consequence of Stravinsky's evolution is that we get from him, year after year, music of amazing freshness and mastery—wonderful new works of art.

STRAVINSKY'S WORK TABLE

C. F. Ramuz

Stravinsky's writing table resembled the instrument stand of a surgeon. . . . The bottles of different colored inks set out according to rank; each had its little role in the grand affirmation of a superior order. They were ranged together with rubber erasers of various kinds and sizes, all sorts of shining steel objects, rulers, eradicators, penknives, drawing pens, not to mention a kind of instrument with wheels Stravinsky had invented for drawing staves. St. Thomas' phrase comes to mind: "Beauty is the splendor of order." Order alone, though, is not enough, it must shed light. Here was an order which did enlighten, by its reflection of an inner clarity. This clarity revealed itself too in all those large pages covered with writing made more complex, persuasive and demanding by means of various inks, blue, green, red, black—two kinds of black, ordinary and Chinese—each having its own place, meaning and special utility. One ink was for notes, another for the first text, a third for the second, still others for titles, and a special one for the various written indications that go into a score. The bars were drawn with a ruler and errors carefully removed with a steel eraser.

Page by page, note by note, stroke by stroke, all those great sheets . . . were filled from top to bottom. . . . They became an impressive mass of black ovals or slightly larger white ones with their stems joined

Translated by Dollie Pierre Chareau, from *Souvenirs sur Igor Stravinsky*, written in 1917 by C. F. Ramuz. Copyright, 1946, Mermod, Switzerland.

Stravinsky at Work. California, 1945

in bunches or ranged in a line like fruit on an espalier. . . . All that had been noise, all the tremendous notes, for example, struck on the cymbalon with the felt or leather mallets, the small and the large, the hard, the soft; all that had been drum-beats, or sounds issuing from the piano or the violin; all that had been sung or shouted, that had been discussed, had been ideas, feelings, sensations, that had revolved first in one head then in another, then in the air between them—which now were fixed, no longer to be shifted—all had become a series of immovable points on paper, transformed by immobility into silence, a silence rich and already straining to restore to the world what it now contained.

———

Carlos Chavez

Le Sacre was in its day a famous scandal. Audiences everywhere were taken completely by surprise. Such music had never been heard before. It appeared to be without logic, idea, or any sense whatever. People were shocked, even disgusted by its oddness.

Only a few—the real musicians—discovered a notion of order, harmony, organization, composition, of character itself, in this music, so radically different from any written before. But the majority did not understand how one could have the courage to affirm that *Le Sacre* was

Martha Graham as the Virgin in *Le Sacre du Printemps.*
Massine-Roerich. New York, 1930

music at all. Even ten years later, in Carnegie Hall, I remember the general air of bewildered distaste at the performance Monteux gave with the Boston Symphony.

Since the 'twenties, however, a growing familiarity with this work, through performance or phonograph record, has made its inherent strength known to everyone. Now, thirty-five years after its premiere, no one dares raise his voice against *Le Sacre*. It is accepted as one of the most extraordinary pieces of music of all time. Clearly it marks the beginning of the career of a great master, whose continuous and powerful activity sets him apart on an eminence all his own. No one now contests Stravinsky's greatness.

But even today many people who like music, some scholars, some eminent musicians, feel that Stravinsky's genius no longer has the dazzling glow of his first period of *L'Oiseau*, *Petrouchka*, *Le Sacre*.

With an air of sadness they lament the premature twilight of his creative power, explaining his return-to-Bach, his interest in Pergolesi, Verdi, Rossini and Tchaikovsky as expressions of mechanized activity in place of original invention.

Two or three years ago, in a California city, a famous violinist told me the following story: He wished to enlarge his repertory, but felt discouraged on viewing the recent concerti for his instrument. He approached Stravinsky. "Of course," he explained, "I wanted something that would have the attractiveness of the *best* Stravinsky. So I told him I thought that in the literature for the violin there ought to be a work corresponding to the admirable music of *L'Oiseau*, *Petrouchka* and *Le Sacre*. . . . Well, Stravinsky did not finally receive my commission, since he answered drily that he was not interested in decadent music."

All new, that is, authentically new music, is received at first with deafness. The public is too lazy to accept immediately new ways of enjoying art, it is not ready to increase its own capacity to enjoy or understand.

Like the distinguished violinist, many people would prefer Stravinsky if he went on forever writing *L'Oiseau*, *Petrouchka*, *Le Sacre* with new titles perhaps. Lack of curiosity and imagination prevents their enjoyment of an *Apollon*, a *Baiser de la Fée*, or a *Symphony in C*. Unwilling to exert themselves even a little, they cannot explore the new worlds he opens. And since he fails to give what they want, they blame him for a disappointment which reflects only their own inadequacy.

The reasons for not liking the new symphony are exactly the same as for not understanding *Le Sacre*. *Le Sacre* was as new in 1913 as the symphony is today. It held no more elements of surprise for the public of the time. But nowadays, people do not make public scandals by shouting. Instead they whisper about the decay of the great master.

In any case it is not Stravinsky who suffers. The loss is theirs. For his music has a surpassing vitality. Its continuity is that of a great creative mind. Each new work is truly new, being at the same time the logical result of those that precede it and of all music existing in the past.

Alert to all influences, Stravinsky receives and dominates them, only to reaffirm more and more his own personality. He is a living proof that authentic genius does not, indeed cannot, evade external influence but always absorbs and masters it.

EARLY YEARS

Pierre Monteux

My first meeting with Stravinsky took place in 1911 when I was guest conductor of the Diaghilev Ballet Russe. Stravinsky, outstanding among the new composers of the modern school, had just achieved his first success with *L'Oiseau de Feu*. We met when I conducted the world premiere of his second ballet, *Petrouchka*. *Petrouchka* was an immense success. In the field of ballet many still consider it Stravinsky's masterpiece.

One day in 1912, after I had become the regular conductor for the Ballet Russe, Diaghilev summoned me to a tiny rehearsal room in a theatre of Monte Carlo where the Ballet was at that time appearing. We were to hear Stravinsky run through the score of his new work, *Le Sacre du Printemps*.

With only Diaghilev and myself as audience, Stravinsky sat down to play a piano reduction of the entire score. Before he got very far I was convinced he was raving mad. Heard this way, without the color of the orchestra which is one of its greatest distinctions, the crudity of the rhythm was emphasized, its stark primitiveness underlined. The very walls resounded as Stravinsky pounded away, occasionally stamping his feet and jumping up and down to accentuate the force of the music. Not that it needed such emphasis.

I was more astounded by Stravinsky's performance than shocked by the score itself. My only comment at the end was that such music would surely cause a scandal. However, the same instinct that had prompted me to recognize his genius made me realize that in this ballet he was far, far in advance of his time and that while the public might not accept it, musicians would delight in the new, weird though logical expression of dissonance.

Le Sacre du Printemps was presented in 1913 at the Théâtre des Champs-Elysées in Paris, and cause a scandal it certainly did. The audience remained quiet for the first two minutes. Then came boos and catcalls from the gallery, soon after from the lower floors. Neighbors began to hit each other over the head with fists, canes or whatever came to hand. Soon this anger was concentrated against the dancers, and then, more particularly, against the orchestra, the direct perpetrator of the musical crime. Everything available was tossed in our direction, but we continued to play on. The end of the performance was greeted by the arrival of gendarmes. Stravinsky had disappeared through a window backstage, to wander disconsolately along the streets of Paris.

A year later I suggested to Stravinsky that he arrange a concert version of the *Sacre* for the Concerts Monteux at the Casino de Paris. Anxious himself to prove a few points, he readily agreed. The presentation was an instant success.

Time has caught up with Stravinsky. Now he is recognized as one of the great of the world. He has advanced musical expression tremendously and almost every contemporary composer owes him an acknowledged debt.

———

STRAVINSKY'S REDISCOVERIES

Walter Piston

Few present day composers can safely disclaim the influence of Igor Stravinsky upon their development and certainly few would wish to. The presence of a genius of the first rank is always something to be thankful for and to profit by, like any other fine experience. The changes in style and manner brought about by Stravinsky's music in the early 'twenties do not seem to me, however, to be the most important results of his influence. In those days all the young composers saw to it that their compositions had some of the characteristics of rhythm and dissonance they so admired in *Les Noces* and *Le Sacre*. I remember taking a work to Paul Dukas and feeling secretly a little proud of his comment, "*C'est Stravinskique*," although I knew perfectly well that the good *maître* did not approve. But these earmarks were in the main superficial details of imitation, not signs of the larger and more significant influence of Stravinsky on the art of music.

It was my good fortune to become personally acquainted with Stravinsky when he visited Harvard as the Charles Eliot Norton Professor in 1939–40. Besides his series of lectures, now published under the title *Poétique Musicale*, he held extremely rewarding meetings with the students, discussing their music and his own. In the course of a talk about *Oedipus Rex*, at one of these meetings, an observation that he made threw a bright light on a most important aspect of his artistic ideals. He said, "How happy I was when I discovered that chord!" Some of us were puzzled, because the chord, known in common harmonic terms as a D-major triad, appeared neither new nor complex. But it became evident that Stravinsky regarded every chord as an individual sonority, having many attributes above and beyond the tones selected from a scale or altered this way and that. The particular and marvelous combination of tones in question owed its unique character to the exact distribution of the tones in relation to the spaces between them, to the exact placing of the instrumental voices in reference to the special sound of a given note on a given instrument, to the dynamic level indicated, and to the precise moment of sounding of the chord.

When we realize that such precision marks Stravinsky's approach to every technical and esthetic problem connected with musical composition, we begin to see why his influence has been inescapable, why his music has been so great a stimulation to other composers. He has recreated, revalued, and refreshed all branches of the art—harmony, melody, rhythm, form, color, orchestration—and in the process he has given us a store of significant, inspiring, and lasting works. To these influences in the domain of technique we must add the example of Stravinsky's unswerving faithfulness to his ideals, his unwillingness to sacrifice one particle of principle to gain success or critical approval. These are qualities one should take for granted in men of high achievement, but in a time when publicity so often substitutes for truth, integrity is a force for good that cannot be too eagerly recognized or too often acclaimed.

THIRTY-SEVEN YEARS

Darius Milhaud

The great privilege of musicians now in their fifties is to have witnessed at first hand all the works of Stravinsky as he produced them.

In 1910 I was present at the premiere of *L'Oiseau de Feu*. After that we had to wait a year, more or less, to hear the next work.

Every year thereafter Diaghilev brought us the new Stravinsky— always different, always unexpected, always more than exciting. From *L'Oiseau de Feu* to the extraordinary *Orpheus* that Stravinsky played on his piano for my wife and me in Hollywood in 1947 every work has its weight, its deep resounding in our soul. Each time different problems are involved, and each time their solutions are achieved in masterly fashion.

I am thankful to be fifty-five years old and to have been able, for thirty-seven of them, to observe this prodigious production.

While teaching at Mills College I had a tremendous experience which increased my admiration for Stravinsky (if that were indeed pos-

Stravinsky, Madeleine and Darius Milhaud, Nadia Boulanger.
California, 1944

sible). I established a course of study in his music, and every Tuesday
I analyzed, one after the other, all his works. To go through these
scores, written between 1910 and 1947, is a real comfort for a musician
and his students, united in their love of art.

A NOTE ON VARIETY

Leonard Bernstein

Stravinsky has been a basic factor in my musical life ever since the red-
letter day when, at the age of fifteen, I heard my first piece of "modern
music"—*Le Sacre du Printemps*. From that feverishly emotional experience until my recent quite different one of recording *L'Histoire* and the
Octuor, the music of this astounding composer has grown increasingly
dear to me—even indispensable; and, incredibly, always fresher.

That he is a master is universally accepted. That his originality is
unrivalled (for an eminently *tonal* composer) we all realize. That his
influence has been formidable goes without saying. But to me as a conductor, his unique value is his fabulous *variety*.

I venture to say that there is no other contemporary composer from whose works one could fashion an entire program for a regular symphony audience. But such a program is surprisingly simple to make and a delight to conduct.

The variety is in itself manifold. There is a stylistic variety which makes each work sound new and different from the last. We are treated to a series of historical flashes ranging from Pergolesi to Tchaikovsky. We can select from a continuum that runs from irony or pure balletic entertainment to the most moving profundity. There are all degrees of complexity, from the *Norwegian Moods* to *Petrouchka*. And there is infinite variety of orchestral sonority. No two pieces ever sound really alike in timbre.

This last quality is what mystifies me. Especially because the personal trade-marks are always present: the niceties of his doublings, the disposition of his chords, his unconventional use of strings, his addiction to wind instruments, and his uncompromisingly lean clarity, even in the earlier works. He combines, in his handling of the orchestral groups, a stability which always guarantees a "sound," with an almost fussy way of casting subtle lights and shadows by means of meticulous detail. Yet one never tires of his sonorities.

The same fact obtains in respect to his choral music. *Les Noces*, the *Psaumes*, *Oedipus*, and *Perséphone* are all as different as can be. And even such apparently similar chamber works as *L'Histoire* and the *Octuor* sound like night and day when heard on the same program.

This welcome capacity for variety extends even into the theatre. A series of Stravinsky ballets in one lump would be a joy, and a constantly fresh surprise. One could open with *Apollon*, follow with *Le Baiser de la Fée*, and finish with *Petrouchka*. Or one could combine *Danses Concertantes*, *Les Noces*, and *L'Oiseau*. I doubt if any other composer of any period could offer us these possibilities, be he Lully, Tchaikovsky or Copland.

Stravinsky's variety is a treasure, and a conductor's boon. In an audience, I am a fan; as a composer, a humble admirer; as a worker in the theatre, an observing student. But as a conductor, I am eternally grateful.

———

THE COMPOSER'S DEBT

Vittorio Rieti

Whether it takes form as opera or ballet, the music theatre always faces a special problem: Shall the drama come first, or the music?

Stravinsky's answer, in a period weighted all on the side of drama by post-Wagnerian influence, has been unwaveringly for music. This is one of many reasons why, as a composer, I am grateful to him. His attitude encourages those of us who, dealing with a particular subject, believe that music should not be subservient to the literary mechanism, that it has the power to recreate action in its own pure terms. I will not dwell longer on this much debated point, nor, for the sake of argument, evoke the ghosts of Monteverdi and Verdi, Debussy and Tchaikovsky. It is enough to show Stravinsky's position and be thankful for it.

But although we are at the moment chiefly concerned with Stravinsky's gifts to the theatre, I want to seize the opportunity to thank him for a great many other substantial benefactions: his emphasis on the qualities of the artisan within the artist; his demonstration that the tonal system is not dead; his faith in Apollo; his non-belief in Wotan; his worship of the classics; his love of Italian music; the readiness to forsake his own patterns once he feels them exhausted, thereby avoiding a systematic self-pursuit into decadence. And, yes—special thanks are due him for not asking us to swallow crescendo porridge, pedal sauce and rubato marmalade.

———

THE FINAL TRIUMPH

William Schuman

At his tender historical age Stravinsky already belongs to music. For some time now it has been possible to admire the work of this master in the normal fashion of the general consumer of music, i.e., without the aid of lobbying. This fact is not often recognized by the cultists whose modus vivendi is celebrating Stravinsky's famous cause. But Stravinsky's music has proven more powerful than all the combined verbal forces that have been pitted against and for it. Extra-musical forces have the power to retard or accelerate the course of destiny for a creative artist, but not, I think, to change it. Let the cultists rejoice, then, for they have succeeded in accelerating the acceptance of Stravinsky; we are all in their debt. They are also free to pursue other useful occupations!

Even composers are now far enough removed from the heat of the battle to admire him without being directly and overwhelmingly influenced by his style(s). Stravinsky's music has been a major factor in the emergence and increasing general use of a new musical speech. This synthesizes in fresh tonal idioms the speech of composers seemingly disparate in esthetics, as is graphically shown in the work of some of our younger Americans. While it is true that in a few instances their work stems directly from Stravinsky, most of them now are influenced indirectly through a composer of a generation in between. The result of this greater distance is to be found not only in a more interesting language than a mere imitation could ever be, but in a less technical and more musical and humane understanding of Stravinsky's enormous contribution.

Young composers today are not impressed in the same way with Stravinsky's earlier experimental works as the group who attended the birth. These younger men are not impressed in the same way with the excitingly original concept of Stravinsky's orchestra or rhythms or forms. They are not impressed in the same way because Stravinsky for them is an accepted fact and not a celebrated cause.

It is not the existence of a cult which gives Stravinsky his place in the great line. His real triumph is his complete victory over the thoughtful musicians of his time. No composer with such a conquest to his credit could ever long remain without a large and understanding listening public.

WORKING WITH STRAVINSKY

Lincoln Kirstein

When we decided to ask Stravinsky to write for the American Ballet there was no question of providing the composer with even the suggestion of a subject. And, as a matter of fact, we were ignorant of his choice for six months after the contract was signed.

The orchestration and piano score of *Jeu de Cartes* (The Card Party, Ballet in Three Deals) were finished simultaneously in November, 1936, and we received the score on December second. The title page also credits M. Malaiev, a friend of Stravinsky's painter son, Theodore, with aid in contriving the action. The scene is a card table at a gaming house, and the dancers are members of the pack. The choreography must closely follow indications of composer and librettist because the action, in numbered paragraphs, refers to equivalents in the score itself.

Three deals of straight poker are demonstrated, played literally according to Hoyle. Sudden apparitions of the Joker, to whom these rules do not apply, destroy the logical suits of the three hands. At the end of each deal giant fingers of otherwise invisible croupiers remove the rejected cards.

The musical opening of each deal is a short processional (march, polonaise or waltz) which introduces the shuffling of the pack. For the card play—deals, passes, bets—there are group dancers, solo variations and finales according to the familiar usage of classic ballet.

The music is dry, brilliant, melodic and extremely complex in its rhythmic pattern, a synthesis of purely creative yet evocative passages, balanced by fragments definitely reminiscent of Rossini, Delibes, Johann Strauss, Pugni, Ravel, Stravinsky's *Capriccio*, and jazz in general. The score is so compact, so various, and so willful that either the chore-

Reprinted from *Modern Music*, Vol. XIV, No. 3. Copyright 1937.

Stravinsky, Lincoln Kir-
stein and Alice Halicka.
New York, 1937

ography must be its exact parallel in quality or else it had better be
presented as a concert piece.

Stravinsky, it seems, expended his utmost care on the skeletal choreographic plan and on his music. George Balanchine brought all his theatrical information and the resources of his knowledge of the classic
dance into designing the dances, which were about half done when Stravinsky first saw them. (Stravinsky and Balanchine had worked together
on previous occasions. In 1924 Balanchine, fresh from Russia, presented
Le Rossignol as a ballet, and in 1928 he created the Diaghilev premiere
of *Apollon Musagètes*.)

When Stravinsky saw the first two deals of *Jeu de Cartes*, he expressed an enthusiasm, an interest and a criticism which was as courtly
as it was terrifying. The ballet, as with so many Russians, is deep in his
blood. It is not only a question of childhood memories of interminable
performances at the Maryinsky Theatre, or of the famous works he has
himself composed or seen. Stravinsky completely understands the vocabulary of classic dancing. He has more than the capacity to criticize
individual choreographic fragments, doubled fouettés here, a series of
brisés accelerated or retarded, or points of style as in the elimination of
pirouettes from a ballet which is primarily non-plastic but one-dimen-
sional and card-like. His is the profound stage instinct of an amateur of
the dance, the "amateur" whose attitude is so professional that it seems
merely an accident that he is not himself a dancer.

Jeu de Cartes. Balanchine-Sharaff. William Dollar as the Joker. New York, 1937

The creation of *Jeu de Cartes* was a complete collaboration. Stravinsky would appear punctually at rehearsals and stay on for six hours. In the evenings he would take the pianist home with him and work further on the tempi. He always came meticulously apparalled in suede shoes, marvelous checked suits, beautiful ties—the small but perfect dandy, an elegant Parisian version of London tailoring. During successive run-throughs of the ballet he would slap his knee like a metronome for the dancers, then suddenly interrupt everything, rise and, gesticulating rapidly to emphasize his points, suggest a change. This was never offered tentatively but with the considered authority of complete information.

Thus at the end of the first deal, where Balanchine had worked out a display of the dancers in a fan-like pattern to simulate cards held in the hand, Stravinsky decided there was too great a prodigality of choreographic invention. Instead of so much variety in the pictures he preferred a repetition of the most effective groupings.

It is not that he is tyrannical or capricious. But when he writes dance music he literally sees its ultimate visual realization, and when his score is to be achieved in action he is in a position to instruct the choreographer not by suggesting a general atmosphere but with a detailed and exactly plotted plan. For all questions of interpretation within his indicated limits of personal style or private preference, he has a respectful generosity. He is helpful in a wholly practical sense. For example, realizing that when he conducts the performances he may have a tendency to accelerate the indicated metronomic tempi, he ordered the accompanist to play faster than heretofore for rehearsals, to take up a possible slack when the ballet is danced on the stage itself. On another occasion he composed some additional music to allow for a further development in the choreography.

As with the music and dancing, so with the costumes and scenery. Before his arrival we had been attracted by the idea of using a set of medieval playing cards and adapting them in all their subtle color and odd fancy to the stage. Forty costumes and the complete scenery were designed before he arrived in America. Upon seeing the sketches Stravinsky insisted they would place the work in a definite period and evoke a decorative quality not present in his music. He called for the banal colors of a deck of ordinary cards, forms and details so simple as to be immediately recognizable. Stravinsky's precise delimitation gave Irene Sharaff, the designer, a new orientation, and strangely enough a new freedom for clarity and originality.

Stravinsky has about him the slightly disconcerting concentration of a research professor or a newspaper editor, the serious preoccupation of a man who has so many interrelated activities to keep straight and in smooth running order that he finds it necessary to employ a laconic, if fatherly and final politeness. The effect is all the more odd coming from a man who is at once so small in stature, and who, at least from his photographs, appears not to have changed a bit in twenty-five years. When he speaks he seems to be the paternal mouthpiece of a permanent organization or institution rather than a creative individual.

We had difficulties of course in choosing from all his repertory two other ballets to complete the evening with *Jeu de Cartes*. . . . At length *Apollon* was selected, because both Balanchine and Stravinsky wished to present it in the choreography of its Paris presentation.

The third ballet, *Le Baiser de la Fée*, first produced in 1928 for Ida Rubinstein by Nijinsky, had never been seen in North America. This is less a salad of Tchaikovsky quotations, as is frequently assumed, than a projection of the method which Tchaikovsky created, of framing the classic dance as ritual drama. It is less a recapturing of the epoch of *Giselle* than it is another facet of the creative attitude of Stravinsky.

Stravinsky is a composer who meets each problem within the tradition of the theatre, a tradition which he has helped to create, in which he resides, and onto which he continually builds.

STRAVINSKY'S OWN STORY

L'OISEAU DE FEU

Fokine; Pavlova; Karsavina

Diaghilev . . . asked me to write the music for *L'Oiseau de Feu* for the Russian Ballet season at the Paris Opera House in the spring of 1910. . . . The ballet had just undergone a great transformation owing to the advent of a young ballet master, Fokine, and the flowering of a whole bouquet of artists full of talent and originality: Pavlova, Karsavina, Nijinsky. Notwithstanding all my admiration for the classical ballet and its great master, Marius Petipa, I could not resist the intoxication produced by . . . *Les Danses du Prince Igor* or *Carnaval*, the only two of Fokine's productions that I had so far seen.

Diaghilev, with his company and collaborators, preceded me, so that when I joined them [in Paris] rehearsals were in full swing. Fokine elaborated the scenario, having worked at his choreography with burning devotion, the more so because he had fallen in love with the Russian fairy story. The casting was not what I had intended. Pavlova, with her slim angular figure, had seemed to me infinitely better suited to the role of the fairy bird than Karsavina, with her gentle feminine charm, for whom I had intended the part of the captive princess. Though circumstances had decided otherwise than I had planned, I had no cause for complaint, since Karsavina's rendering of the bird's part was perfect, and that beautiful and gracious artist had a brilliant success in it. . . .

However, the choreography of this ballet always seemed to me to be complicated and overburdened with plastic detail, so that the artists felt, and still feel even now, great difficulty in co-ordinating their steps and gestures with the music. This often led to an unpleasant discordance between the movements of the dance and the imperative demands that the measure of the music imposed.

Excerpts from *Stravinsky: An Autobiography*, by Igor Stravinsky. Copyright 1936 by Simon and Schuster, Inc.

L'Oiseau de Feu. Fokine-Golovine.
Fokine and Karsavina. Paris, 1910

. . . In the sphere of choreography I [still] prefer, for example, the vigor of the *Danses du Prince Igor*, with their clear-cut and positive lines, to the somewhat detached designs of *L'Oiseau de Feu*.

PETROUCHKA

Nijinsky's dancing; Benois; Fokine

Before tackling *Le Sacre du Printemps* . . . I wanted to refresh myself by composing an orchestral piece in which the piano would play the most important part—a sort of *Konzertstück*. . . . I had in mind . . . a puppet, suddenly endowed with life, exasperating the patience of the orchestra with diabolical cascades of arpeggios. The orchestra in turn

Stravinsky and Adolf Bolm during a rehearsal of *Petrouchka*. New York, 1943. (Photograph: Eileen Darby)

Petrouchka. Fokine-Benois. The Moor's Cell. Paris, 1912

retaliates with menacing trumpet blasts. The outcome is a terrific noise which reaches its climax and ends in the sorrowful and querulous collapse of the poor puppet. . . .

Soon afterwards Diaghilev came to visit me at Clarens, where I was staying. . . . I played him the piece I had just composed and which later became the second scene of *Petrouchka*. He was so much pleased with it that he would not leave it alone and began persuading me to develop the theme of the puppet's sufferings and make it into a whole ballet. . . . By mutual agreement, Diaghilev entrusted the whole decor of the ballet, both the scenery and the costumes, to Benois. . . .

I should like at this point to pay heartfelt homage to Vaslav Nijinsky's unsurpassed rendering of the role of Petrouchka. The perfection with which he became the very incarnation of this character was all the more remarkable because the purely saltatory work in which he usually excelled was in this case definitely dominated by dramatic action, music and gesture. The beauty of the ballet was greatly enhanced by the richness of the artistic setting that Benois had created for it. My faithful interpreter, Karsavina, swore to me that she would never relinquish her part as the dancer, which she adored. But it was a pity that the movements of the crowd had been neglected. I mean that they were left to the arbitrary improvisation of the performers instead of being choreographically regulated in accordance with the clearly defined exigencies of the music. I regret it all the more because the *danses d'ensemble* of the coachmen, nurses, and mummers and the solo dances must be regarded as Fokine's finest creations.

ON CHOREOGRAPHY

Le Sacre: Nijinsky's failure

One day, when I was finishing the last pages of *L'Oiseau de Feu* in St. Petersburg, I had a fleeting vision which came as a complete surprise. . . . I saw in imagination a solemn pagan rite: sage elders, seated in a circle, watched a young girl dance herself to death. They were sacrificing her to propitiate the god of spring. Such was the theme of *Le Sacre du Printemps*. . . . This vision . . . I at once described to my friend, Nicholas Roerich, he being a painter who had specialized in pagan sub-

Petrouchka. Stravinsky and Nijinsky. Paris, 1911

jects. He welcomed my inspiration with enthusiasm, and became my collaborator in this creation. . . .

Diaghilev made up his mind that year [1912] that he would spare no effort to make a choreographer of Nijinsky. I do not know whether he really believed in his choreographic gifts, or whether he thought that his talented dancing . . . indicated that he would show equal talent as a ballet master. . . .

To be perfectly frank . . . the idea of working with Nijinsky filled me with misgiving, notwithstanding our friendliness and my great admiration for his talent as dancer and mime. His ignorance of the most elementary notions of music was flagrant. The poor boy knew nothing of music. He could neither read it nor play any instrument, and his reactions were expressed in banal phrases or the repetition of what he had heard others say. As one was unable to discover any individual impressions, one began to doubt whether he had any. These lacunae were so serious that his plastic vision, often of great beauty, could not compensate for them. My apprehension can be readily understood, but I had no choice in the matter. . . .

Nijinsky began by demanding such a fantastic number of rehearsals that it was physically impossible to give them to him. It will not be difficult to understand why he wanted so many, when I say that in trying to explain to him the construction of my work, in general outline and in detail, I discovered that I should achieve nothing until I had taught him the very rudiments of music: values—semibreve, minim, crochet, quaver, etc.—bars, rhythm, tempo, and so on. He had the greatest difficulty in remembering any of this. Nor was that all. When, in listening to music, he contemplated movements, it was always necessary to remind him that he must make them accord with the tempo, its divisions and values. It was an exasperating task, and we advanced at a snail's pace. . . .

He appeared to be quite unconscious both of his inadequacy and of the fact that he had been given a role which, to put it shortly, he was incapable of filling. . . . Seeing that he was losing prestige with the company but was strongly upheld by Diaghilev, he became presumptuous, capricious, and unmanageable. . . .

Le Sacre du Printemps was given on May 28 [1913]. . . . During the whole performance I was at Nijinsky's side in the wings. He was

Vaslav Nijinsky. New York,
1915

standing on a chair, screaming "sixteen, seventeen, eighteen"—they had their own method of counting to keep time. Naturally the poor dancers could hear nothing by reason of the row in the auditorium and the sound of their own dance steps. I had to hold Nijinsky by his clothes, for he was furious, and ready to dash onto the stage at any moment. . . . Diaghilev kept ordering the electricians to turn the lights on or off, hoping in that way to put a stop to the noise. That is all I can remember about the first performance. . . .

Now, after the lapse of more than twenty years, it is naturally difficult for me to recall in any detail the choreography of the *Sacre* without being influenced by the admiration it met in the set known as the *avant-garde*—ready, as always, to welcome as a new discovery anything that differs, be it ever so little, from the *déjà vu*. But what struck me then, and still strikes me most, about the choreography, was and is Nijinsky's lack of consciousness of what he was doing in creating it. . . . What

Le Sacre du Printemps. Massine-
Roerich. Sokolova. 1920

the choreography expressed was a very labored and barren effort rather than a plastic realization flowing simply and naturally from what the music demanded. How far it all was from what I had desired!

In composing the *Sacre* I had imagined the spectacular part of the performance as a series of rhythmic mass movements of the greatest simplicity which would have an instantaneous effect on the audience, with no superfluous details or complications such as would suggest effort. The only solo was to be the sacrificial dance at the end of the piece. The music of that dance, clear and well defined, demanded a corresponding choreography—simple and easy to understand. But there again, although he had grasped the dramatic significance of the dance, Nijinsky was incapable of giving intelligible form to its essence, and complicated it either by clumsiness or lack of understanding. For it is undeniably clumsy to slow down the tempo of the music in order to compose complicated steps which cannot be danced in the tempo prescribed. Many choreographers have that fault, but I have never known any who erred in that respect to the same degree as Nijinsky. . . .

In 1920, Diaghilev gave a new production of *Le Sacre du Printemps* at the Théâtre des Champs-Elysées.

Nijinsky's absence—he had been interned for some years—and the impossibility of remembering his overburdened, complicated, and confused choreography, gave us the idea of recreating it in a more living form, and the work was entrusted to Leonide Massine.

The young ballet master accomplished his task with unquestionable talent.

He certainly put order and understanding into his dance compositions. There were even moments of great beauty in the group movements when the plastic expression was in perfect accord with the music, and, above all, in the sacrificial dance so brilliantly executed by Lydia Sokolova that it still lives in the memory of everyone who saw it.

I must say, however, that notwithstanding its striking qualities and the fact that the new production flowed out of the music and was not, as the first had been, imposed on it, Massine's composition had in places something forced and artificial about it. This defect frequently arises, as choreographers are fond of cutting up a rhythmic episode of the music into fragments, of working up each fragment separately, and then sticking the fragments together. By reason of this dissection, the choreographic line, which should coincide with that of the music, rarely does so, and the results are deplorable; the choreographer can never by such methods obtain a plastic rendering of the musical phrase. In putting together these small units (choreographical bars) he obtains, it is true, a total which agrees with the length of a given musical fragment, but he achieves nothing more. The music is not adequately represented by a mere addition sum, but demands from choreography an organic equivalent of its own proportions. Moreover, this procedure on the part of the choreographer reacts unfavorably on the music itself, preventing the listener from recognizing the musical fragment choreographed. I speak from experience, because my music has frequently suffered from this deplorable method.

PULCINELLA

Joys and trials of collaboration; Massine; Picasso

The success of *The Good-humored Ladies,* with Scarlatti's music, had suggested the idea of producing something to the music of another illustrious Italian, Pergolesi, whom . . . I liked and admired immensely.

Frequent conferences with Diaghilev, Picasso, and Massine were necessitated by the task before me—which was to write a ballet for a definite scenario, with scenes differing in character but following each other in ordered sequence. . . . Our conferences were very often far from peaceable; frequent disagreements arose, and our meetings occasionally ended in stormy scenes.

Sometimes the costumes failed to come up to Diaghilev's expectations; sometimes my orchestration disappointed him. Massine composed his choreography from a piano arrangement made from the orchestral score and sent piecemeal to him by me as I finished each part. As a result of this it often happened that when I was shown certain steps and movements that had been decided upon I saw to my horror that in character and importance they in no wise corresponded to the very modest possibilities of my small chamber orchestra. They had wanted, and looked for, something quite different from my score, something it could not give. The choreography had, therefore, to be altered and adapted to

Pulcinella. Design for curtain by Picasso. 1920.

the volume of my music, and that caused them no little annoyance, though they realized that there was no other solution.

Although all this was tiring, I enjoyed taking part in a task which ended in a real success. *Pulcinella* is one of those productions, and they are rare, where everything harmonizes, where all the elements—subjects, music, dancing, and artistic setting—form a coherent and homogeneous whole. As for the choreography, with the possible exception of a few episodes that it had not been possible to change, it is one of Massine's finest creations, so fully has he assimilated the spirit of the Neapolitan theatre. In addition, his own performance in the title role was above all praise. As for Picasso, he worked miracles, and I find it difficult to decide what was most enchanting—the coloring, the design, or the amazing inventiveness of this remarkable man.

RENARD AND MAVRA

Bronislava Nijinska

[I made] several visits to Monte Carlo, where the choreography of *Renard* was being created by Bronislava Nijinska, sister of the famous dancer and herself an excellent dancer endowed with a profoundly artistic nature, and, in contrast to her brother, gifted with a real talent for choreographic creation.

Diaghilev and I also confided to her the direction of the artists acting in *Mavra* as regards plastic and movement. She had marvellous ideas, which were unfortunately balked by the inability of the singers to sub-

Bronislava Nijinska. Drawing by
Cocteau. 1924

Renard. Lifar-Larionov. Paris, 1929

ject themselves to a technique and discipline in the practice of which they were unversed.

It was quite different with *Renard*. I still deeply regret that the production, which gave me the greatest satisfaction both musically (the music was under the direction of Ansermet) and scenically (the scenery and costumes were by Larionov and were one of his greatest successes), has never been revived in that form. Nijinska had admirably seized the spirit of its mountebank buffoonery. She displayed such . . . ingenuity, so many fine points, and so much satirical verve that the effect was irresistible. She, herself, in the part of Renard, was an unforgettable figure.

LES NOCES

A Difference with Diaghilev

I must say that the stage production of *Les Noces*, though obviously one of talent, did not correspond with my original plan. I had pictured to myself something quite different. . . .

The spectacle should have been a divertissement, and that is what I wanted to call it. It was not my intention to reproduce the ritual of peasant weddings, and I paid little heed to ethnographical considerations. My idea was to compose a sort of scenic ceremony, using as I liked those ritualistic elements so abundantly provided by village customs which had been established for centuries in the celebration of Russian marriages. I took my inspiration from those customs, but reserved to myself the right to use them with absolute freedom. . . . I wanted all my instrumental apparatus to be visible . . . a participant in the whole theatrical action. For this reason, I wished to place the orchestra on the stage itself, letting the actors move on the space remaining free. The fact that the artists in the scene would uniformly wear costumes of a Russian character while the musicians would be in evening dress not only did not embarrass me, but, on the contrary, was perfectly in keeping with my idea of divertissement of the masquerade type.

But Diaghilev had no sympathy with my wishes. And when, to convince him, I pointed out how successful the plan had been in *L'Histoire du Soldat*, I only stimulated his furious resistance because he could not bear *L'Histoire*.

Apollon Musagètes. Balanchine-Bauchant. Doubrovska, Lifar and Tchernicheva. Paris, 1928

Apollon Musagètes. Design by Bauchant. 1928

APOLLON

For strings and melody; Balanchine

About this time [1927] I was asked by the Congressional Library at Washington to compose a ballet for a festival of contemporary music. . . .

I chose as theme, Apollo Musagetes—that is, Apollo as the master of the Muses, inspiring each of them with her own art. I reduced their number to three, selecting from among them Calliope, Polyhymnia and Terpsichore as being the most characteristic representatives of choreographic art. . . .

When, in my admiration for the beauty of line in classical dancing, I dreamed of a ballet of this kind, I had specially in my thoughts what is known as the "white ballet," in which to my mind the very essence of this art reveals itself in all its purity. I found that the absence of many-colored effects and of all superfluities produced a wonderful freshness. This inspired me to write music of an analogous character. It seemed to me that diatonic composition was the most appropriate for this purpose, and the austerity of its style determined what my instrumental ensemble must be. I at once set aside the ordinary orchestra because of its heterogeneity, with its groups of string, wood, brass, and percussion instruments. I also discarded ensembles of wood and brass . . . and I chose strings. . . .

The taste for melody *per se* having been lost, it was no longer cultivated for its own sake, and there was therefore no criterion by which its value could be assessed. It seemed to me that it was not only timely but urgent to turn once more to the cultivation of this element from a purely musical point of view. That is why I was so much attracted by the idea of writing music in which everything should revolve about the melodic principle. And then the pleasure of immersing oneself again in the multisonorous euphony of strings and making it penetrate even the furthest fibres of the polyphonic web! And how could the unadorned design of the classical dance be better expressed than by the flow of melody as it expands in the sustained psalmody of strings? . . .

Balanchine, who had already given proof of great proficiency and imagination in his ballet productions, notably in the charming *Barabau* by Rieti, had designed for the choreography of *Apollon* groups, movements and lines of great dignity and plastic elegance as inspired by the beauty of classical forms. As a thorough musician—he had studied at the St. Petersburg Conservatory—he had had no difficulty in grasping the smallest details of my music, and his beautiful choreography clearly expressed my meaning. As for the dancers, they were beyond all praise. The graceful Nikitina with her purity of line alternating with the enchanting Danilova in the role of Terpsichore; Tchernicheva and Doubrovska, those custodians of the best classical tradition; finally, Serge Lifar, then still quite young, conscientious, natural, spontaneous, and full of serious enthusiasm for his art—all these formed an unforgettable company.

But my satisfaction was less complete in the matter of costume and decor, in which I did not see eye to eye with Diaghilev. As I have already said, I had pictured it to myself as danced in short white ballet skirts in a severely conventionalized theatrical landscape devoid of all fantastic embellishment such as would have been out of keeping with my primary conception. But Diaghilev, afraid of the extreme simplicity of my idea, and always on the lookout for something new, wished to enhance the spectacular side, and entrusted scenery and costumes to a provincial painter, little known to the Paris public—André Bauchant, who, in his remote village, indulged in a genre of painting somewhat in the style of the *douanier* Rousseau. What he produced was interesting, but, as I had expected, it in no way suited my ideas.

HOMAGE TO TCHAIKOVSKY

Le Baiser; Nijinska again

[At the end of 1927] I received from Mme Ida Rubinstein a proposal to compose a ballet for her repertory. The painter Alexandre Benois . . . submitted two plans, one of which seemed very likely to attract me. The idea was that I should compose something inspired by the music of Tchaikovsky. . . .

As I was free to choose both the subject and scenario of the ballet, I began to search for them, in view of the characteristic trend of Tchaikovsky's music, in the literature of the nineteenth century. . . .

In turning over the pages of Andersen, with which I was fairly familiar, I came across a story I had completely forgotten, which struck me as being the very thing for the idea that I wanted to express. It was the very beautiful story known to us as *The Ice Maiden*. . . .

Although I gave full liberty to painter and choreographer in the staging of my composition, my innermost desire was that it should be presented in classical form, after the manner of *Apollon*. I pictured all the fantastic roles as danced in white ballet skirts, and the rustic scenes as taking place in a Swiss landscape, with some of the performers dressed in the manner of early tourists and mingling with the friendly villagers in the good old theatrical tradition. . . . I found some of the scenes successful and worthy of Nijinska's talent. But there was, on the other hand, a good deal of which I could not approve, and which, had I been present at the moment of their composition, I should have tried to get altered. But it was now too late for any interference on my part, and I had, whether I liked it or not, to leave things as they were. It is hardly surprising in these circumstances that the choreography of *Le Baiser de la Fée* left me cold.

LANGUAGE AND MUSIC

Oedipus Rex, Cocteau; Perséphone, Gide

As soon as my *Sérénade* was finished [1925] I felt the necessity for undertaking something big. I had in mind an opera or an oratorio on some universally familiar subject. My idea was that in that way I could concentrate the whole attention of the audience, undistracted by the story, on the music itself, which would thus become both word and action. . . .

I have always considered that a special language . . . was required for subjects touching on the sublime. That is why . . . I finally selected Latin. The choice had the great advantage of giving me a medium not dead, but turned to stone and so monumentalized as to have become immune from all risk of vulgarization. My mind continued to dwell on my new work, and I decided to take my subject from the familiar myths of ancient Greece. I thought that I could not do better for my libretto than to appeal to my old friend, Jean Cocteau . . . I had just seen his *Antigone*, and had been much struck by the manner in which he had handled the

Oedipus Rex. Design by Dühlberg for Klemperer's production. Berlin, 1928

ancient myth and presented it in modern guise. Cocteau's stagecraft is excellent. He has a sense of values and an eye and feeling for detail. . . . This applies alike to the movements of the actors, the setting, the costumes, and, indeed, all the accessories.

Cocteau was delighted with my idea, and set to work at once. We were in complete agreement in choosing *Oedipus Rex* as the subject. We kept our plans secret, wishing to give Diaghilev a surprise for the twentieth anniversary of his theatrical activities, which was to be celebrated in the spring of 1927.

At the opening of the New Year I received from Cocteau the first part of his final version of *Oedipus* in the Latin translation of Jean Danielou. . . . All my expectations were fully justified. I could not have wished for a more perfect text, or one that better suited my requirements.

The knowledge of Latin, which I had acquired at school, but neglected, alas! for many years, began to revive as I plunged into the libretto, and, with the help of the French version, I rapidly familiarized

Drawing by Larionov. Stravinsky, Diaghilev, Cocteau, Satie

myself with it. As I had fully anticipated, the events and characters of the great tragedy came to life wonderfully in this language, and, thanks to it, assumed a statuesque plasticity and a stately bearing entirely in keeping with the majesty of the ancient legend.

What a joy it is to compose music to a language of convention, almost of ritual, the very nature of which imposes a lofty dignity! One no longer feels dominated by the phrase, the literal meaning of the words. Cast in an immutable mold which adequately expresses their value, they do not require any further commentary. The text thus becomes purely phonetic material for the composer. He can dissect it at will and concentrate all his attention on its primary constituent element —that is to say, on the syllable. Was not this method of treating the text that of the old masters of austere style? This, too, has for centuries been the Church's attitude towards music, and has prevented it from falling into sentimentalism, and consequently into individualism.

At the beginning of 1933 Mme Ida Rubinstein had inquired whether

Perséphone. Design by Barsacq for Ida Rubinstein's
production. Paris, 1934

Ida Rubinstein as Perséphone.
Drawing by Barsacq. 1934

I would consent to write the music for a poem by André Gide, which he had planned before the war . . . Gide joined me at Wiesbaden. He showed me his poem which was taken from the superb Homeric hymn to Demeter . . . expressed his willingness to make any modification . . . required by the music, and under such conditions an agreement was quickly reached. . . .

With the exception of two melodies for some lines by Verlaine, this was my first experience of composing music for French words. I had always been afraid of the difficulties of French prosody. Although I had been living in France for twenty years, and had spoken the language from childhood, I had until now hesitated to use it in my music. I now decided to try my hand, and was more and more pleased as my work proceeded. What I most enjoyed was syllabifying the music to French, as I had done for Russian in *Les Noces*, and for Latin in *Oedipus Rex*.

ON CLASSICAL BALLET

[In London] I saw, as presented by Diaghilev, that *chef d'oeuvre* of Tchaikovsky and Petipa, *The Sleeping Beauty*. Diaghilev had worked at it passionately and lovingly, and once more displayed his profound knowledge of the art of ballet. He put all his soul, all his strength, into it, in the most disinterested way. . . .

It was a real joy to me to take part in this creation, not only for love of Tchaikovsky but also because of my profound admiration for classical ballet, which, in its very essence, by the beauty of its *ordonnance* and the aristocratic austerity of its forms, so closely corresponds to my conception of art. For here, in classical dancing, I see the triumph of studied conception over vagueness, of the rule over the haphazard. I am thus brought face to face with the eternal conflict in art between the Apollonian and the Dionysian principle. The latter assumes ecstasy to be the final goal—that is to say, the losing of oneself—whereas art demands above all the full consciousness of the artist. There can, therefore, be no doubt as to my choice between the two. And if I appreciate so highly the value of classical ballet, it is not simply a matter of taste on my part, but because I see exactly in it the perfect expression of the Apollonian principle.

THE DEATH OF DIAGHILEV

1929 [was] a year overshadowed by a great and grievous event—the passing of Diaghilev. . . .

At the beginning of my career he was the first to single me out for encouragement. . . . Not only did he like my music and believe in my development, but he did his utmost to make the public appreciate me. He was genuinely attracted by what I was then writing, and it gave him real pleasure to produce my work, and, indeed, to force it on the more rebellious of my listeners. . . . These feelings of his, and the zeal which characterized them, naturally evoked in me a reciprocal sense of gratitude, deep attachment, and admiration for his sensitive comprehension,

Russian caricature of Diaghilev. 1909

his ardent enthusiasm, and the indomitable fire with which he put things into practice.

Our friendship, which lasted for almost twenty years, was, alas! marked from time to time by conflicts. . . . It is obvious that my relations with Diaghilev could not but undergo a certain change in the later years in view of the broadening of the field of my personal and independent activities, and of the fact that my collaboration with the Russian Ballet had lost the continuity it had earlier enjoyed. There was less affinity than before in our ideas and opinions, which, as time went on, frequently developed in divergent directions. "Modernism" at any price, cloaking a fear of not being in the vanguard; the search for something sensational; uncertainty as to what line to take—these things wrapped Diaghilev in a morbid atmosphere of painful gropings. All this prevented me from being in sympathy with everything he did, and this made us less frank in our relations with each other. Rather than upset him, I evaded these questions, especially as my arguments would have served no useful purpose. . . .

My last contact with Diaghilev was in connection with *Renard*, which he was recreating for his spring season at the Théâtre Sarah Bernhardt. Without entering here into a discussion of the new setting, I must say that I missed the first version created by Nijinska in 1922, of which I have already spoken.

After that season in Paris I saw him only once—casually, and at a distance on the platform of the Gare du Nord, where we were both taking the train for London. Six weeks later the news of his death reached me at Echarvines, where I was spending the summer as I had done the year before. . . .

At the moment . . . I gave myself up to my grief, mourning a friend, a brother, whom I should never see again. . . .

It is only today, with the passing of the years, that one begins to realize everywhere and in everything what a terrible void was created by the disappearance of this colossal figure, whose greatness can only be measured by the fact that it is impossible to replace him. The truth of the matter is that everything that is original is irreplaceable. I recall this fine phrase of the painter, Constantine Korovine: "I thank you," he said one day to Diaghilev, "I thank you for being alive."

AN ALBUM OF DATES
AND PICTURES

IGOR STRAVINSKY, 1882—

A few important dates in his life and career

EARLY YEARS IN RUSSIA

1882 June 17 (St. Igor's Day)—Born at Oranienbaum near St. Petersburg

1903 Meeting with Rimsky-Korsakov who later became his teacher

1906 Marriage to Catherine Nossenko, his first cousin

1908 Premiere of *First Symphony*, St. Petersburg, his first public performance

FIRST DIAGHILEV PERIOD

1910 Premiere of *L'Oiseau de Feu* in Paris, first ballet commissioned by Diaghilev

1911 Premiere of *Petrouchka*, Paris

1913 Premiere of *Le Sacre du Printemps*, Paris

1914 Premiere of first opera, *Le Rossignol*, commissioned by Diaghilev, Paris. Last visit to Russia, on the eve of World War I

RESIDENCE IN SWITZERLAND

1914–20 Composition of works on Russian folk material

1918 Premiere of *L'Histoire du Soldat* at Lausanne

RESIDENCE IN FRANCE

1920 Premiere of *Pulcinella*, ballet after Pergolesi, in Paris

1922 Premiere of *Renard* in Paris

1922 *Mavra*, second opera, a chamber work, produced in Paris

1923 Premiere of *Les Noces*, Paris

1925 First visit to America; conducts New York Philharmonic Symphony

1927 *Oedipus Rex*, oratorio, premiere in Paris

1928 *Le Baiser de la Fée*, Paris premiere of Ida Rubinstein production

1928 April—Premiere of *Apollon* in Washington, D. C., first American commission

1930   Premiere in Brussels of *Symphonie de Psaumes*, dedicated to the Boston Symphony Orchestra

1934   Premiere of *Perséphone*, Paris. Ida Rubinstein production

1934   June 10—Becomes French citizen

1937   Conducts premiere of *Jeu de Cartes* in New York, second American ballet commission

1939   Death of Stravinsky's wife in Paris

RESIDENCE IN THE UNITED STATES

1939   Fall and Winter—Fills Charles Eliot Norton Chair of Poetry at Harvard

1940   Marries Vera Soudeikina at Bedford, Mass.

1942   Conducts premiere of *Danses Concertantes* with the Janssen Symphony Orchestra at Los Angeles

1942   *Circus Polka* given first performance in New York at Ringling Bros. Circus

1944   *Scènes de Ballet* premiere, New York, in Billy Rose production, *The Seven Lively Arts*

1945   Becomes American citizen

1947   Begins collaboration with W. H. Auden on opera, *The Rake's Progress*

1948   Premiere in New York of *Orpheus*, Ballet Society production

1948   The *Mass*, first performance at La Scala in Milan

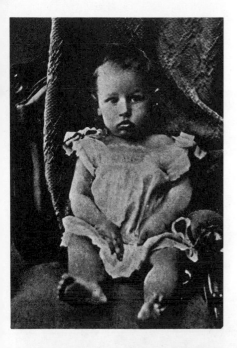

Russia, 1883

Paris, 1911

California, 1947

Group photographed at the Ritz Hotel, Madrid, 1916. Seated, left to right: Massine, Del Campo, Ansermet, Diaghilev, Salvador, Stravinsky, de Falla. Bolm

Stravinsky, Fokine and Karsavina during a rehearsal of *L'Oiseau de Feu.* 1910

L'Histoire du Soldat. Drawing of the collaborators by Auberjonois. Ramuz, Stravinsky, Ansermet, Pitoev and the artist. 1918

New York, 1939. (Photo-
graph: Eric Schaal)

New York, 1947. (Photograph:
Adrian Siegel)

Stravinsky at his home in California. 1947

Stravinsky with his son, Soulima, and grandson. California, 1948. (Photograph: Ernest Beadle [courtesy of *Harper's Bazaar*])

STAGE PRODUCTIONS OF STRAVINSKY'S WORKS

The following tables list the original productions of Stravinsky's theatre works—"original" meaning new choreography or decor or both. Many of these (notably Diaghilev's) were mounted at different times and places. Such repetitions are not listed here. Notations are occasionally incomplete, due to the present difficulty of obtaining accurate information from European sources.

Directly below each title the date of composition, the publishing house and the approximate duration of performance are given. The production column lists the sponsoring individual, group, or institution. Abbreviations have been made where necessary: I.S.C.M. for International Society for Contemporary Music; N.C.A.S.F. for National Council of American-Soviet Friendship, Inc.; Ballet Russe de M.C. for Ballet Russe de Monte Carlo.

WORKS COMPOSED AND STAGED AS BALLETS

Production	Choreography	Decor	Place & Date
L'OISEAU DE FEU			
1909–10, Schott, 45 minutes			
Diaghilev	Fokine	Golovine	Paris, 1910
Maryinsky	Lopoukhov	Golovine	Petrograd, 1921
Diaghilev	Fokine	Gontcharova	London, 1926
Staatsoper	Maudrik	Dobrouen	Berlin, 1927
Royal Opera	Steier	Grunewald	Stockholm, 1927
Royal Theatre	Kaj Smith	(unverified)	Copenhagen, 1928
Stadttheater	Loeser	Jurgens	Düsseldorf, 1929
Opernhaus	Hermann	(unverified)	Königsberg, 1929
Teatro Colon	Fokine	Bilibine	Buenos Aires, 1931
Stadttheater	Zehnpfennig	Clemens	Zurich, 1933
(unverified)	Kratina	Zircher	Karlsruhe, 1937
Stadttheater	Macke	Clemens	Zurich, 1940
Hollywood Bowl	Bolm	Remisov	Hollywood, 1940
Ballet Theatre	Bolm	Chagall	New York, 1945
Staatsoper	Luipart	Loghi	Munich, 1947
PETROUCHKA			
1910–11, Edition Russe, 42-3 minutes			
Diaghilev	Fokine	Benois	Paris, 1911
Metropolitan	Bolm	Wenger	New York, 1919
Maryinsky	Leontiev	Benois	Petrograd, 1920
Staatsoper	Kroller	Pasetti	Berlin, 1919 (?)
Metropolitan	Bolm	Soudeikine	New York, 1924
La Scala	(unverified)	Depero	Milan, 1927

Production	Choreography	Decor	Place & Date
Opernhaus	Georgi	Kirsta	Hanover, 1927
Staatsoper	Terpis	Dühlberg	Berlin, 1928
(unverified)	Furstenau	(unverified)	Karlsruhe, 1928
Staatsoper	Jooss	Heckroth	Essen, 1930
Royal Opera	Algo	Jon-And	Stockholm, 1932
Teatro Grande	Nijinska	(unverified)	Breschia, 1933
Teatro Reale	Petrov	Benois	Rome, 1934
Staatstheater	Gerzers	(unverified)	Stuttgart, 1937
Stadttheater	Macke	Clemens & Stockar	Zurich, 1939
Teatro Reale	Milloss	N. Benois	Rome, 1942
Stadttheater	Macke	T. Stravinsky	Zurich, 1943
Royal Opera	Gué	Runsten	Stockholm, 1943
Staatsoper	Hanka	Kautsky	Vienna, 1947
Staatsoper	Gzovsky	(unverified)	Berlin, 1947

LE SACRE DU PRINTEMPS
1912–13, Edition Russe, 30 minutes

Diaghilev	Nijinsky	Roerich	Paris, 1913
Diaghilev	Massine	Roerich	Paris, 1920
League of Composers	Massine (new)	Roerich (new)	New York, 1930
Teatro Colon	Romanov	Acosta	Buenos Aires, 1932
Teatro dell' Opera	Milloss	Benois	Rome, 1941

PULCINELLA
1919, Chester, 30 minutes

Diaghilev	Massine	Picasso	Paris, 1920
Maryinsky	Lopoukhov	Dmitriev	Petrograd, 1925
Stadttheater	Georgi	Kirsta	Hanover, 1927 (?)
Royal Opera	Steier	Grunewald	Stockholm, 1927
Teatro Colon	Romanov	Franco	Buenos Aires, 1928
Duke of Reuss' Theater	Wiener	(unverified)	Gera, 1928
Opernhaus	Galpern	Blanke	Cologne, 1929
Opernhaus	Jooss	Heckroth	Essen, 1932
New York Music Guild	Novikov	Paepcke & Badger	Chicago, 1933
Teatro Quirino	Romanov	Severini	Rome, 1938
Teatro Reale	Milloss	N. Benois	Rome, 1942

LES DEUX POLICHINELLES

Coliseum	Woiczikowsky	(unverified)	London, 1935

COMMEDIA BALLETICA

Ballet Russe de M.C.	Bolender	Davidson	New York, 1945

RENARD
1916–17, Chester, 15 minutes

Diaghilev	Nijinska	Larionov	Paris, 1922
Maryinsky	Lopoukhov	Dmitriev	Petrograd, 1927
Diaghilev	Lifar	Larionov	Paris, 1929

Production	Choreography	Decor	Place & Date
Teatro delle Arti	Thieben	Prampolini	Rome, 1941
Ballet Society	Balanchine	Francés	New York, 1947

LES NOCES
1917–23, Chester, 23 minutes

Diaghilev	Nijinska	Gontcharova	Paris, 1923
Teatro Colon	Nijinska	Franco	Buenos Aires, 1926
League of Composers	Anderson-Ivantzova	Soudeikine	New York, 1929
Städt. Theater	Hermann	Jacobs	Königsberg, 1929
Teatro delle Arti	Alanova	Prampolini	Rome, 1942
Stadttheater	Macke	Otto	Zurich, 1948

APOLLON MUSAGETES
1927–28, Edition Russe, 28 minutes

Coolidge	Bolm	Remisov	Washington, 1928
Diaghilev	Balanchine	Bauchant	Paris, 1928
Royal Opera	Balanchine	Abel	Copenhagen, 1931
American Ballet	Balanchine	Chaney	New York, 1937
American Ballet	Balanchine	Santa Rosa	Rio de Janeiro, 1941
Teatro delle Arti	Milloss	Prampolini	Rome, 1941
Teatro Colon	Balanchine	Tchelitchev	Buenos Aires, 1942

LE BAISER DE LA FEE
1928, Edition Russe, 45 minutes

Rubinstein	Nijinska	Benois	Paris, 1928
Teatro Colon	Nijinska	Basaldua	Buenos Aires, 1933
Sadlers Wells	Ashton	Fedorovitch	London, 1935
American Ballet	Balanchine	Halicka	New York, 1937
Staatsoper	Maudrik	Novikov	Berlin, 1937

JEU DE CARTES
1936, Schott, 20 minutes

American Ballet	Balanchine	Sharaff	New York, 1937
Staatsoper	Kratina	Kratina	Dresden, 1937
Stadttheater	Mlakar	Clemens	Zurich, 1938
Ballet des Champs-Elysées	Charrat	Roy	Paris, 1945
Teatro Colon	Wallman	Basaldua	Buenos Aires, 1948
Teatro dell' Opera	Milloss	Guttuso	Rome, 1948

CIRCUS POLKA
1942, Associated Music Publishers, 4 minutes

Ringling Brothers	Balanchine	Bel Geddes	New York, 1942

SCENES DE BALLET
1944, Chappell & Co., 15 minutes

Billy Rose	Dolin	Dupont	New York, 1944
Covent Garden	Ashton	Beaurepaire	London, 1948

Production	Choreography	Decor	Place & Date
ORPHEUS			
1947, Boosey & Hawkes, 31 minutes			
Ballet Society	Balanchine	Noguchi	New York, 1948
Festival of Contemp.			
Music	Milloss	Clerici	Venice, 1948
Théâtre des Champs-			
Elysées	Lichine	Mayo	Paris, 1948

BALLETS SET TO OPERA OR CONCERT MUSIC

FEU D'ARTIFICE			
1907–08, Schott, 4 minutes			
Diaghilev	(none)	Balla	Rome, 1918
LE CHANT DU ROSSIGNOL			
1917, Edition Russe, 20 minutes			
Diaghilev	Massine	Matisse	Paris, 1920
Diaghilev	Balanchine	Matisse	Paris, 1925
Städt. Oper	Maudrik	Dobrouen	Berlin, 1929
TWO SUITES FOR SMALL ORCHESTRA			
1921 and 1925, Chester, 4 minutes each			
DEUX PETITES SUITES			
Stadttheater	Loeser	Jurgens	Düsseldorf, 1929
PETITES SUITES			
Stadium Concerts	Limon	Limon	New York, 1936
CAPRICES			
Teatro delle Arti	Milloss	Scialoja	Rome, 1943
AFTERTHOUGHTS			
N.C.A.S.F.	Robbins	Robbins	New York, 1946
BALUSTRADE (Violin Concerto)			
1931, Schott, 20 minutes			
De Basil	Balanchine	Tchelitchev.	New York, 1944
DANSES CONCERTANTES			
1941–42, Associated Music Publishers, 19 minutes			
Ballet Russe de M.C.	Balanchine	Berman	New York, 1944
ELEGIE (for viola)			
1944, Chappell & Co., 6 minutes			
School of American			
Ballet	Balanchine	(none)	New York, 1945
CAPRICCIO (for piano and orchestra)			
1929, Edition Russe, 20 minutes			
La Scala	Massine	N. Benois	Milan, 1947

WORKS COMPOSED AND STAGED AS OPERA OR ORATORIO

PRODUCTION	STAGE ACTION	DECOR	PLACE & DATE

LE ROSSIGNOL (Story and text: Andersen–Mitoussov)
1908–14, Edition Russe, 45 minutes

Diaghilev	Romanov	Benois	Paris, 1914
Diaghilev	(unverified)	Depero	Rome, 1916
Maryinsky	Myerhold	Golovine	Petrograd, 1918
Metropolitan	Thewman	Soudeikine	New York, 1926
La Scala	(unverified)	(unverified)	Milan, 1926
Staatsoper	(unverified)	N. Benois	Berlin, 1927
Teatro dell' Opera	(unverified)	Urbano	Rome, 1928

L'HISTOIRE DU SOLDAT (Story and text: C. F. Ramuz)
1918, Chester, 25 minutes

W. Reinhart	Pitoev	Auberjonois	Lausanne, 1918
Art Theatre	(unverified)	Galitzine & Soudeikine	London, 1927
Städt. Bühnen	Jooss	Heckroth	Münster, 1927
League of Composers	Ito	Oenslager	New York, 1928
Kroll Oper	Ebert	(unverified)	Berlin, 1929
Stadttheater	(unverified)	Jurgens	Düsseldorf, 1930
I.S.C.M.	Page	Remisov	Chicago, 1931
Salabianca	Scherchen	(unverified)	Florence, 1935
Teatro delle Arti	Fulchignoni	Guttuso	Rome, 1940
Ballet Club	Cranko	(unverified)	Cape Town, 1944
I.S.C.M.	Kahl	Tryggvadottir	New York, 1946
Théâtre des Champs-Elysées	Roulet	Faravel	Paris, 1946
Staatsoper	Jokisch	Hartmann	Munich, 1946
Teatro Colon	Wallman	Basaldua	Buenos Aires, 1948
I.S.C.M.	Kahl	Kiesler	New York, 1948

MAVRA (Story and text: Pushkin–Kochno)
1921–22, Edition Russe, 30 minutes

Diaghilev	Nijinska	Survage	Paris, 1922
Kroll Oper	(unverified)	(unverified)	Berlin, 1928
Philadelphia Orchestra	Graf	Soudeikine	Philadelphia, 1934
Teatro dell' Opera	Milloss	Abkasi	Rome, 1942
La Scala	Marchioro	N. Benois	Milan, 1948

OEDIPUS REX (Story and text: Sophocles–Cocteau–Danielou)
1926–27, Edition Russe, 55 minutes

Staatsoper	Wallerstein	Rollers	Vienna, 1928
Kroll Oper	Klemperer	Dühlberg	Berlin, 1928
Stadttheater	Schram	(unverified)	Düsseldorf, 1928

PRODUCTION	STAGE ACTION	DECOR	PLACE & DATE
Opernhaus	Schultze-Dornberg	Neher	Essen, 1928
Staatsoper	Cohen	Heckroth	Essen, 1930
Teatro Colon	(unverified)	Dühlberg	Buenos Aires, 1931
League of Composers	Stokowski	Jones & Bufano	New York, 1931
Stadttheater	Zimmerman	Clemens	Zurich, 1934
Teatro Comunale	Celestini	Valente	Florence, 1937
Teatro Colon	(unverified)	Basaldua	Buenos Aires, 1942
La Scala	Savinio	N. Benois	Milan, 1948
Juilliard	Cohen	Kiesler	New York, 1949

PERSEPHONE (Story and text: André Gide)
1933–34, Edition Russe, 45 minutes

Rubinstein	Jooss	Barsacq	Paris, 1934
Teatro Colon	(unverified)	(unverified)	Buenos Aires, 1936
Landestheater	(unverified)	(unverified)	Braunchschweig, 1938
Stadttheater	Macke	Otto	Zurich, 1948

RECORDINGS OF MUSIC BY IGOR STRAVINSKY

This list, compiled early in 1949, includes all recordings made of Stravinsky's music, from the earliest to the most recent. Dates following the titles are those of composition. Dates of recording, when known, are given immediately after the notations about performing artists.

Starred record numbers indicate rare items either out of print or not generally available. Daggers indicate that the number is not that of the original recording, but refers to a later release.

PASTORALE, 1908
Arrangement, 1923
　　Dushkin (violin) with Paris Woodwind Quartet, 1933　　†Col. LF129
　　Stokowski and Philadelphia Orchestra Quartet, 1939　　Vic. 1998
　　Szigeti (violin) with Woodwind Quartet, 1948　　Col. 72495D
　　Szigeti (violin) and Magaloff (piano), 1934　　†Col. 7304M

FEU D'ARTIFICE, 1908
　　Kleiber and Berlin Philharmonic Orchestra, 1930　　†Ultra. F14385
　　Pierné and Colonne Orchestra, 1930　　*Parlo. R20109
　　de Sabata and E.I.A.R. Symphony Orchestra, 1938　　Cetra PP60009
　　Stravinsky and N. Y. Philharmonic Symphony Orchestra
　　　1947　　Col. 12459D
　　Defauw and Chicago Symphony Orchestra, 1947　　Vic. 11 9447

ETUDES OP. 7 (for piano), 1908
Nos. 3 and 4
　　Soulima Stravinsky, 1940　　Boîte à Musique 27
No. 4
　　Moiseivitch, 1938　　Gramo. C2998

L'OISEAU DE FEU, 1910
　　Stravinsky and Symphony Orchestra, 1929　　†Col. M 115
Arrangement, 1919
　　Stokowski and Philadelphia Orchestra, 1936　　†Vic. M 291
　　Stokowski and All-American Youth Orchestra, 1941　　Col. M 446
　　Stokowski and N.B.C. Symphony Orchestra, 1943　　Vic. M 933
　　Galliera and Philharmonia Orchestra, 1947　　Col. DCX70-2
Arrangement, 1945
　　Stravinsky and N. Y. Philharmonic Symphony Orchestra,
　　　1947　　Col. M 653
Other Arrangements
　　Kleiber and Berlin State Opera Orchestra, 1930　　*Odeon 6816, 6762-3
　　Fried and Berlin Philharmonic Orchestra　　Polydor 516650-1

Defosse and Russian Ballet Orchestra   *Ed. Bell x501-2
Ansermet and London Philharmonic Orchestra, 1947   Decca ED30

Excerpts
Coates and London Symphony Orchestra, 1928   *H.M.V. D1510
Stokowski and Philadelphia Orchestra   *H.M.V. D1427

Berceuse
Dushkin (violin) and Stravinsky (piano), 1934   *Col. LF130
Milstein (violin) and Mittman (piano), 1938   *Col. 17115D
Pierné and Colonne Orchestra   Odeon 123525

PETROUCHKA, 1911
Coates and London Symphony Orchestra, 1928   *H.M.V. D1521-4
Stokowski and Philadelphia Orchestra, 1939   Vic. M 575
Ansermet and London Philharmonic Orchestra, 1946   †Decca ED2

Excerpts
Stravinsky and Symphony Orchestra, 1928   *Col. L2173-5
Koussevitzky and Boston Symphony Orchestra, 1929   *H.M.V. D2094-6
Stravinsky and N. Y. Philharmonic Symphony Orchestra, 1940   *Col. 11389-90D
Defosse and Russian Ballet Orchestra   *Ed. Bell x503-4
Monteux and Symphony Orchestra   *Gramo. W1008-11
Pierné and Colonne Orchestra   *Odeon 123577-9
Doyen (piano) with Poulet Orchestra   *Decca F2337
Stravinsky and N.Y. Philharmonic Symphony Orchestra   Col. X177

Danse Russe
Arrau (piano)   *Polydor 90025
Luboshutz and Nemenoff (two pianos)   *Vic. 2096
Dushkin (violin) and Stravinsky (piano)   *Col. LF129
Szigeti (violin) and Magaloff (piano)   *Col. LB38
Y. Nat (piano), 1928   *Col. D13114
Magaloff (piano)   Rad. RZ3033
Gimpel (violin) and Balsam (piano), 1947   Vox 616
Goehr and Symphony Orchestra   Vic. C30: G-C2925

THREE JAPANESE LYRICS, 1913
Rosing (one lyric only)   *Vocalion

LE SACRE DU PRINTEMPS, 1913
Stravinsky and Symphony Orchestra, 1929   *Col. D15213-7
Stokowski and Philadelphia Orchestra, 1930   †Vic. M 74
Stravinsky and Symphony Orchestra   Col. LX119-23
Stravinsky and N. Y. Philharmonic Symphony Orchestra, 1940   Col. M 417
Monteux and Symphony Orchestra   *Fr. H.M.V. W1016-9
Monteux and San Francisco Symphony Orchestra, 1946   Vic. M 1052
Van Beinum and Amsterdam Orchestra, 1948   Decca K 1727-30

THREE PIECES FOR STRING QUARTET, 1914
Krettly Quartet   *Col. D15182
Gordon String Quartet, 1948   Concert Hall Soc. B6

LE CHANT DU ROSSIGNOL, 1917
  Goossens and Cincinnati Symphony Orchestra, 1946   Vic. M 1041
  Marche Chinoise
    Coates and London Symphony Orchestra, 1931   *H.M.V. D1932
    Dushkin (violin) and Stravinsky (piano), 1934   *Col. LX383

TILIMBOM, 1917
  Kipnis (bass) and Dougherty (piano), 1940   *Vic. 15894

LES NOCES, 1917
  Stravinsky and Chorus, Soloists, Ensemble, 1934   †Col. M 204
  Arrangement, 1923
    Stravinsky (excerpt of above)   Col. DB 1306

VOLGA BOAT SONG, arranged 1917
  Koussevitzky and Boston Symphony Orchestra, 1939   †Vic. 15364

FIVE EASY PIECES FOR PIANO–FOUR HANDS, 1917
  Gold and Fizdale, 1947   Concert Hall Soc. A6

L'HISTOIRE DU SOLDAT, 1918
  Stravinsky and Paris Ensemble, 1932   †Col. M 184
  Bernstein and Boston Ensemble, 1948   Vic. 12 0136-8

RAGTIME, 1918
  Stravinsky and Ensemble, 1934   *Col. LX382

PIANO RAG-MUSIC, 1919
  Marcelle Meyer, 1926   *H.M.V. D1063
  Stravinsky, 1934   *Col. LX382

PULCINELLA, 1920
  Excerpts
    Stravinsky and Symphony Orchestra, 1933   *Col. LFX289
    Stravinsky and Symphony Orchestra, 1933   *Col. D15126
    Stravinsky and Symphony Orchestra   Col. GQX11064
  Serenata and Scherzino
    Dushkin (violin) and Stravinsky (piano), 1933   *Col. LX290
  Suite Italienne
    Hooton (cello) and Moore (piano), 1940   Decca X263-4

CONCERTINO, 1920
  Hindemith and Amar Quartet, 1922   *Polydor B29056
  Gordon String Quartet, 1948   Concert Hall Soc. B6

SUITE NO. 2, 1921
  Pierné and Colonne Symphony Orchestra, 1930   *Odeon 123667
  Malko and Danish Radio Orchestra, 1948   Gramo. Z297
  Excerpts
    Pierné and Colonne Symphony Orchestra, 1930   *Parlo. R20109

MAVRA, 1922
  Maiden's Song
    Fournier (cello) and Piano, 1944   *H.M.V. DA 4956
    Szigeti (violin) and Stravinsky (piano), 1948   Col. 72495D

OCTUOR, 1923
    Stravinsky and Paris Ensemble, 1933   †Col. X25
    Bernstein and Boston Symphony Players, 1948   †Vic. 12 0129-40

CONCERTO FOR PIANO AND WINDS, 1924
    Soulima Stravinsky (piano) with Oubradous and
      Paris Wind Ensemble, 1945   Gramo. DB11105-6

SERENADE EN LA, 1925
    Stravinsky (piano), 1934   Col. GQ7194-5

APOLLON MUSAGETES, 1927
    Boyd Neel and String Orchestra, 1937   Decca X167-70
    Pas de Deux
    Koussevitzky and Boston Symphony Orchestra, 1929   *H.M.V. D2096

LE BAISER DE LA FEE, 1928
    Divertimento
    Stravinsky and Mexican Symphony Orchestra, 1945   Vic. M 931
    Stravinsky and Victor Orchestra, 1948   Vic. M 1202
    Pas de Deux
    Dorati and London Symphony Orchestra, 1939   *Col. D 949

CAPRICCIO, 1929
    Stravinsky (piano) with Ansermet and   †Col. GQX10519-20;
      Straram Orchestra, 1930   GQX10556
    Sanromá (piano) with Koussevitzky and
      Boston Symphony Orchestra, 1940   Vic. M 685

SYMPHONIE DE PSAUMES, 1930
    Stravinsky and Straram Orchestra and Vlassoff Choir,
      1931   †Col. M 162
    Ansermet and London Philharmonic Orchestra and
      Choir, 1948   Decca EDA 52

VIOLIN CONCERTO, 1931
    Dushkin (violin) with Stravinsky and
      Lamoureux Orchestra, 1932   †Vox 173

DUO CONCERTANT, 1932
    Dushkin (violin) and Stravinsky (piano), 1934   *Col. LX290

CONCERTO FOR TWO SOLO PIANOS, 1935
    Appleton and Field, 1949   Vox 634

JEU DE CARTES, 1936
    Stravinsky and Berlin Philharmonic Orchestra, 1938   Tele. SK2460-2

CONCERTO IN E♭: "Dumbarton Oaks," 1938
    Schmidt-Isserstedt and Hamburg Chamber Orchestra,
      1939   Tele. E2994-5
    Stravinsky and Chamber Orchestra, 1947   Keynote DM1

TANGO, 1940
    Vronsky and Babin (two pianos), 1945   †Col. 72084D

DANSES CONCERTANTES, 1942
    Stravinsky and Victor Orchestra, 1948   Vic. M 1234

CIRCUS POLKA, 1942
    Vronsky and Babin (two pianos), 1945   †Col. 72084M

FOUR NORWEGIAN MOODS, 1942
    Stravinsky and N. Y. Philharmonic Symphony Orchestra,
        1946   Col. 12371D

SCHERZO A LA RUSSE, 1944
    Stravinsky and Victor Orchestra, 1948   Vic. M 1234

SONATA FOR TWO PIANOS, 1944
    Gold and Fizdale, 1947   Concert Hall Soc. A6
    Gorini and Lorenzi, 1947   Gramo. DB11308-9

SCENES DE BALLET, 1944
    Stravinsky and N. Y. Philharmonic Symphony Orchestra,
        1945   Col. X 245

BABEL, 1944
    Janssen and Symphony Orchestra and Chorus, 1948   Artist JS10

SYMPHONY IN THREE MOVEMENTS, 1945
    Stravinsky and N. Y. Philharmonic Symphony Orchestra,
        1947   Col. M 680

CONCERTO FOR STRINGS IN D, 1946
    Barbirolli and Hallé Orchestra, 1948   H.M.V. C3733-4

BIBLIOGRAPHY

Compiled by Paul Magriel

This list of over 600 references has been compiled chiefly from sources in the New York Public Library and the Library of Congress, Washington, D. C. Most of the sources are music periodicals and books about music, but all other books and periodicals which discuss Stravinsky or some aspect of his work are also included. Although newspapers contain much relevant information, especially in their reviews of first performances, they are not included because of general inaccessibility.

The list is divided into five sections:
1. Books Devoted to Stravinsky
2. Special Periodical Issues Devoted Wholly to Stravinsky
3. References to Stravinsky in Other Books
4. References to Stravinsky in Periodicals
5. References to Specific Works by Stravinsky

There is no duplication. Thus articles listed in the section *Special Periodical Issues Devoted Wholly to Stravinsky* are not listed again under *References to Stravinsky in Periodicals* or in *References to Specific Works by Stravinsky*.

Abbreviations: Besides the obvious ones for months, volume and number, are p.—page, pp.—pages, Illus.—illustrations, Port.—portrait, Jahrg. and Jaarg. for year.

SAMPLE ENTRY

Dahl, Ingolf—Stravinsky in 1946. *In* Modern Music. Vol. 23, pp. 159-165. Illus. New York, Summer 1946.

Explanation: An article by Ingolf Dahl, entitled *Stravinsky in 1946*, will be found in the magazine Modern Music, published in New York, Summer issue of 1946. The article runs from page 159 through page 165, and is illustrated.

BOOKS DEVOTED TO STRAVINSKY

Armitage, Merle, Editor—Igor Stravinsky, edited by Merle Armitage: articles and critiques by Eugene Goossens, Henry Boys, Olin Downes, Merle

Armitage, Emile Vuillermoz, Louis Danz, José Rodriquez, Manuel Komroff, Jean Cocteau, and Boris de Schloezer. New York, G. Schirmer, 1936. xv-158 pp. illus.

Asaf'ev, Boris—Knigo o Stravinskom. Leningrad, Triton, 1929. 398 pp. port. A work on the composer in Russian. (Asaf'ev writes also under the pseudonym of Glebov.)

Casella, Alfredo—Igor Strawinski. Roma, A. F. Formiggini, 1926. 48 pp. port. Bibliographia, p. 48.

Collaer, Paul—Strawinsky. Bruxelles, Editions "Equilibres," 1931. 163 pp. illus., music.

Contents: Catalogue des oeuvres d'Igor Strawinsky.—Les premières compositions jusqu'à *L'Oiseau du Feu.*—De *Petrouchka* au *Rossignol.*—De *Noces* à *Pulcinella.*—Les oeuvres récentes.

Fleischer, Herbert—Strawinsky. Berlin, Russischer Musik Verlag, 1931. 286 pp. illus., music.

Contents: Die Welt Strawinskys: a. Einwirkungen der Zeit.—b. Das Eingelichte. Das Werk: 1. Das Frühwerk.—2. *Petrushka.*—3. *Frühlingsweihe.*—4. Der Weg zur *Bauernhochzeit.*—5. Russische *Bauernhochzeit.*—6. Der Europäer.—7. *Die Geschichten vom Soldaten.*—8. *Oedipus Rex.*—9. *Capriccio.*—10. *Psalmensymphonie.*

Malipiero, G. F.—Strawinsky. Venezia, Cavallino, 1945. Illus.

Contents: Gli incontri.—La cronache della sua vita (commentario).—Conclusions.—Note biografiche.—Le opere di Igor Strawinsky.

Miniature Essays, Vol. 10—Igor Stravinsky. London, J. & W. Chester, Ltd., 1922. 14 pp. Port. A brief review of the life and career of the composer. Text in French and English.

Paoli, Domenico de—Igor Strawinsky (da L'Oiseau de Feu a Perséphone). Nuova ed. riveduta ed aggiornata. Torino, G. B. Paravia, 1934. 156 pp. illus., music.

Paoli, Domenico de—L'Opera di Strawinsky. Milano, Proprieta Letteraria Riservata, 1931. 160 pp.

An appraisal of the composer's music: *Le Sacre.—Petrouchka.—Le Rossignol.—Renard.—Noces.—L'Histoire du Soldat.—Pulcinella.—Mavra.—Oedipus Rex.—Symphonie de Psaumes.*

Ramuz, C. F.—Noces, et Autres Histoires, d'après le texte russe d'Igor Strawinsky. Illustrations de Théodore Strawinsky. Neuchâtel, Aux Ides et Calendes, 1943.

Ramuz, C. F.—Souvenirs sur Igor Strawinsky. Avec six hors-texte. Paris, Gallimard, Editions de la Nouvelle Revue Française, 1929. 105 pp. illus., music.

Ramuz, C. F.—Souvenirs sur Igor Strawinsky. Portraits et pages manuscrites. Lausanne, Mermod, 1946. 161 pp. illus., music.

Schaeffner, André—Strawinsky. Avec soixante planches hors-texte en héliogravure. Paris, Les Editions Rieder, 1931. 127 pp. illus., music.
Contents: *Petrouchka.—Le Sacre du Printemps.—Le Rossignol* et *Chant du Rossignol.—L'Histoire du Soldat.—Mavra.*—Table chronologique des oeuvres.

Schloezer, Boris de—Igor Strawinsky. Paris, Editions Claude Aveline, 1929. 175 pp.
A critical estimate of the composer's work up to and including *Apollon.*
Contents: 1. Le russe et l'européen.—2. La technique.—3. Le problème du style.—4. Un art classique.

Stravinsky, Igor—Chronicle of My Life. Translated from the French. London, V. Gollancz, 1936. 286 pp. illus.

Stravinsky, Igor—Chroniques de ma Vie; avec six dessins hors-texte. Paris, Denoel et Steele, 1935. 2 vols. illus.

Stravinsky, Igor—Cronicas de mi Vida, con una carta prologo de Victoria Ocampo y un Retrato de Picasso. Buenos Aires, Sur, 1935. 173 pp.
Spanish translation of Chroniques de ma Vie, Vol. 1, by G. de Torre.

Stravinsky, Igor—Erinnerungen. Zürich-Berlin, Atlantis-Verlag, 1937. 227 pp. illus., music.
German translation of Chroniques de ma Vie, by Richard Tungel.

Stravinsky, Igor—Nuevas Cronicas de mi Vida. Buenos Aires, Sur, 1936. 161 pp.
Spanish translation of Vol. 2 of Chroniques de ma Vie, by L. Hurtado.

Stravinsky, Igor—Poétique Musicale. Avec un portrait de l'auteur par Picasso. Dijon, J. B. Janin, 1945. 166 pp.
Third edition of Poétique Musicale.

Stravinsky, Igor—Poétique Musicale, sous forme de six leçons. Cambridge, Harvard University Press, 1942. 95 pp.
(The Charles Eliot Norton Lectures for 1939–1940.)

Strawinsky, Igor—Poetics of Music, in the Form of Six Lessons. Translated by Arthur Knodel and Ingolf Dahl. Cambridge, Harvard University Press, 1947. 142 pp. illus.
Contents: Preface by Darius Milhaud. 1. Getting acquainted.—2. The phenomenon of music.—3. The composition of music.—4. Musical typology.—5. The avatars of Russian music.—6. The performance of music. English version of Poétique Musicale.

Stravinsky, Igor—Stravinsky: An Autobiography. New York, Simon and Schuster, 1936. xxii-290 pp. illus.
"The aim of this volume is to set down a few recollections connected with various periods of my life . . . Rather than a biography it will be

a simple account of important events side by side with facts of minor importance . . ." Author's foreword.

American version of Chroniques de ma Vie.

Stravinsky, Theodore—Le Message d'Igor Stravinsky. S. A. Lausanne, Aux Editions Rouge et Cie, 1949.

Tansman, Alexandre—Igor Stravinsky. Ouvrage enriché de dix-sept hors-texte. Paris, Amiot-Dumont, 1948. 309 pp. illus., music.

Contents: Prise de vue.—Stravinsky et le phénomène musical.—Discipline et attitude.—Typologie créatrice et mise en oeuvre.—Vie et oeuvre d'Igor Stravinsky.

White, Eric Walter—Stravinsky, a Critical Survey. London, J. Lehmann, 1947. 192 pp. illus., music.

White, Eric Walter—Stravinsky; a Critical Survey. New York, Philosophical Library, 1948. 192 pp. illus., music.

Contents: 1. The apprentice years (Russia, 1882–1910). 2. Success and scandal (France, Switzerland and Russia, 1910–1914). 3. Exile (Vaud, 1914–1920). 4. Composer, conductor, performer (France, 1920–1928). 5. The naturalized Frenchman (France, 1928–1934). 6. The United States of America.

American edition of the preceding.

White, Eric Walter—Stravinsky's Sacrifice to Apollo. London, Leonard & Virginia Woolf, 1930. vii-159 pp.

A general outline of the composer's life and career to 1930. 1. The romantic period. 2. The neo-classical period.

SPECIAL PERIODICAL ISSUES DEVOTED WHOLLY TO STRAVINSKY

Cahiers de Belgique. Année 3, No. 10. Bruxelles, December, 1930. Illus., ports.

Contents: L'Influence de Strawinsky, by Raymond Petit.—Du *Capriccio* à la *Symphonie de Psaumes*, by André Schaeffner.—Strawinsky à Bruxelles, by Arthur Lourié.—La *Symphonie de Psaumes*, by Paul Collaer.—La poésie de Strawinsky, by Franz Hellens.

Contemporaneos. Tomo 5, No. 15. Mexico, August 1929. 32 pp.

El caso Strawinsky.

Contents: Musica y sentiemento.—La musica la accion.—La impersonalidad de Strawinsky.—El periodo Ruso. By Samuel Ramos.

Dance Index. Vol. VI, Nos. 10, 11, 12. New York, 1947. Illus., music. Strawinsky in the Theatre; A Symposium prepared by Minna Lederman. 88 pp.

Neujahreblatt der Allgemeinen Musikgesellschaft in Zürich. No. 121. Zürich & Leipzig, 1933. 38 pp.
Contents: Igor Strawinski, Versuch einer Einführung, by Jacques Handschin.

La Revue Musicale. Année 5, No. 2. Paris, December 1923.
Contents: Igor Strawinsky, by Boris de Schloezer.—Strawinsky, dernière heure, by Jean Cocteau.—Sur Strawinsky, by Michel Georges-Michel.—Strawinsky et nos poètes, by André Coeuroy.—Strawinsky et la danse, by André Levinson.

La Revue Musicale. Numéro Spécial. Igor Strawinsky. Paris, May-June, 1939.
Contents: Critique et thématique, by André Schaeffner.—Démarche de Strawinsky, by Roland-Manuel.—A propos de l'évolution de Strawinsky, by Roger Desormière.—Strawinsky, homme de metiér, by Arthur Honegger.—Igor Strawinsky, le piano et les pianistes, by Alfred Cortot.—A propos d'une première audition d'Igor Strawinsky, by Darius Milhaud.—La notion du temps et la musique, by P. Souvtchinsky.—Igor Strawinsky, législateur du ballet, by Serge Lifar.—Le rythme chez Igor Strawinsky, by Olivier Messiaen.—Hommage à Igor Strawinsky, by Georges Auric.—Invention pure et matière musicale chez Strawinsky, by A. Hoérée.—L'oeuvre du théâtre de Strawinsky, by André Boll.

Tempo. London, Summer 1948. Illus., music. Stravinsky.
Contents: A recollection of Stravinsky, by Tamara Karsavina.—Some memorable occasions, by Cyril W. Beaumont.—Note on the new *Petrouchka*, by Henry Boys.—Stravinsky as a writer, by Eric Walter White.—Recent works examined, by Charles Stuart.

REFERENCES TO STRAVINSKY IN OTHER BOOKS

The American Spectator Year Book. New York, F. A. Stokes, 1934.
Contents include: Stravinsky and Picasso, by Boris de Schloezer, pp. 81-83.

Antheil, George—Bad Boy of Music. New York, Doubleday, Doran & Co., 1945.
Contents include: Igor Stravinsky, pp. 30-40.

Arvey, Verna—Choreographic Music: Music for the Dance. New York, E. P. Dutton, 1941.
Contents include: Igor Stravinsky, pp. 239-259.

Bagar, Robert & Biancolli, Louis—The Concert Companion. A comprehensive guide to symphonic music. New York, Whittlesey House, 1947.
Contents include: Igor Stravinsky, pp. 709-726.

Bakeless, Katherine L.—Story-lives of Great Composers. New York, Frederick A. Stokes, 1940.
Contents include: Igor Stravinsky, pp. 47-58.

Bauer, Marion—Twentieth Century Music. How it developed, how to listen to it. New York, G. P. Putnam Sons, 1947.
Contents include: Stravinsky, the musical barometer, pp. 186-206. Music.

Brahms, Caryl—Footnotes to the Ballet, assembled by Caryl Brahms. London, Lovat Dickson, 1936.
Contents include: The score, by Basil Maine, pp. 135-148. (Estimate of Stravinsky's ballet music.)

Brockway, Wallace, & Weinstock, Herbert—Men of Music: Their lives, times and achievements. New York, Simon & Schuster, 1939.
Contents include: Igor Stravinsky, pp. 557-569.

Brook, Donald—Composers' Gallery: Biographical sketches of contemporary composers. London, Rockcliff, 1946.
Contents include: Igor Stravinsky, pp. 210-218.

Burk, John N., Editor—Philip Hale's Boston Symphony programme notes. New York, Doubleday, Doran & Co., 1935.
Contents include: Igor Stravinsky, pp. 331-338.

Coeuroy, André—Panorama de la Musique Contemporaine. Paris, Kra, 1928.
Contents include: La Leçon de Strawinsky, pp. 17-26.

Copland, Aaron—Our New Music. New York, Whittlesey House, 1941. Contents include: Stravinsky's dynamism, pp. 57-66.

Coton, A. V.—A Prejudice for Ballet. London, Methuen & Co., 1938.
Contents include: *Petrouchka; L'Oiseau de Feu*, pp. 41-53.

Dille, Denijs—Les Maîtres Contemporains de la Musique. Bruxelles, Editions de L'I.N.R., 1936.
Contents include: Igor Stravinsky, pp. 39-46.

Dorian, Frederick—The History of Music in Performance. New York, W. W. Norton & Co., 1942.
Contents include: The objective revolt: Stravinsky, pp. 324-328.

Downes, Olin—Symphonic Masterpieces. New York, The Dial Press, 1935.
Contents include: Igor Stravinsky, pp. 281-294.

Draper, Muriel—Music at Midnight. New York, Harper Bros., 1929.
Contents include: comments on *Le Sacre du Printemps*, pp. 147-150.

Evans, Edwin—Stravinsky—The Firebird and Petrouchka. London, Oxford University Press, 1933. 44 pp. illus.

Ewen, David—Twentieth Century Composers. New York, T. Y. Crowell, 1937.
Contents include: Igor Stravinsky, pp. 3-29.

Ewen, David, Editor—From Bach to Stravinsky. Edited by David Ewen. New York, W. W. Norton, 1933.

Contents include: Stravinsky, by Leonid Sabaneev, pp. 323-340.

Ewen, David, Editor—The Book of Modern Composers. New York, Alfred A. Knopf, 1942.

Contents include: Igor Stravinsky: Personal note, by Janet Flanner, pp. 69-71; The composer speaks, pp. 72-74; Stravinsky, by Alfred J. Swan, pp. 75-82.

Finney, Theodore M.—A History of Music. Revised edition. New York, Harcourt, Brace & Co., 1948.

Contents include: Igor Stravinsky, pp. 573-579.

Gasco, Alberto—Da Cimarosa a Strawinsky; Celebrazioni, critica, spicciola, interviste. Roma, De Santis, 1939.

Contents include: Igor Strawinsky, pp. 435-458.

Graf, Max—Modern Music: Composers and music of our time. New York, Philosophical Library, 1946.

Contents include: The faces of Stravinsky, pp. 241-260.

The Gramophone Shop Encyclopedia of Recorded Music. Third edition. New York, Crown Publishers, 1948.

Contents include: Stravinsky, pp. 517-519.

Gray, Cecil—A Survey of Contemporary Music. Oxford University Press, 1924.

Contents include: Igor Stravinsky, pp. 127-150.

Grout, Donald Jay—A Short History of Opera. New York, Columbia University Press, 1947.

Contents include: National Opera, pp. 478-479.

Hallstrom, John—Relax and Listen: How to enjoy music through records. New York, Rinehart & Co., 1947.

Contents include: Some modern composers, Stravinsky, pp. 179-183.

Hull, Eaglefield—Music; Classical, Romantic and Modern. London, J. M. Dent & Sons, 1927.

Contents include: Stravinsky, pp. 287-292. Port.

Jell, George C.—Masters in Miniature. New York, Barse & Co., 1930.

Contents include: Igor Stravinsky, pp. 257-259.

Johnson, A. E.—The Russian Ballet. Boston & New York, Houghton Mifflin Co., 1913.

Contents include: *The Firebird, Petrouchka, Le Sacre du Printemps.*

Kahan, Salomon—La Emocion de la Musica. Mexico, Editorial Independencia, 1936.

Contents include: *Consagracion de la Primavera*, pp. 193-196. El retroceso de Igor Stravinsky, pp. 197-200.

Lambert, Constant—Music Ho! A study of music in decline. New York, Charles Scribner's Sons, 1934.

Contents include: Diaghileff and Stravinsky as time travellers, pp. 69-77.

Levinson, André—La Danse d'Aujourd'hui. Paris, Duchartre et Van Buggen-houdt, 1929.
Contents include: Stravinsky et la danse théatrale, pp. 75-89.

Lieberson, Goddard, Editor—The Columbia Book of Musical Masterworks. New York, Allen, Towne & Heath, Inc., 1947.
Contents include: Igor Stravinsky, pp. 468-474.

Lifar, Serge—Serge Diaghilev: His life, his work, his legend. New York, G. P. Putnam Sons, 1940.
Contents include: Igor Strawinsky and the ballet, pp. 168-173.

Mason, Daniel Gregory—The Dilemma of American Music. New York, Macmillan, 1928.
Contents include: Stravinsky as a symptom, pp. 111-121.

Mooser, Robert Aloys—Regards sur la Musique Contemporaine, 1921–1946. Lausanne, F. Rouge et Cie., 1946.
Contents include: *Concerto pour piano et orchestre d'harmonie.—Apollon Musagètes.—Noces*, scènes chorégraphiques russes pour soli, choeur, quatre pianos et instruments à percussion.—*Mavra*, opéra-buffe en un acte.—*Jeu de Cartes*, ballet pour orchestre.—*Danses Concertantes*, pour orchestre de chambre.

Nathan, M. Montagu—Contemporary Composers. London, Cecil Palmer & Hayward, 1917.
Contents include: Stravinsky, pp. 113-152.

O'Connell, Charles—The Victor Book of the Symphony. Revised edition. New York, Simon & Schuster, 1941.
Contents include: Igor Stravinsky, pp. 533-547.

Pannain, Guido—Modern Composers, translated with a note by M. R. Bona-via. London, J. M. Dent, 1932.
Contents include: Igor Stravinsky, pp. 35-60.

Pannain, Guido—Musicisti dei Tempi Nuovi. Torino, G. B. Paravia, 1932.
Contents include: Igor Stravinsky, pp. 73-90.

Pijper. Willem—De Quinten-cirkel; Opstellen over muziek. Amsterdam, N.V.E. Querido's Uitgevers-Mij, 1929.
Contents include: Igor Stravinsky, pp. 112-118.

Propert, W. A.—The Russian Ballet. With a preface by Jacques-Emile Blanche. New York, Greenberg, 1932.
Contents include: *Les Noces*, pp. 21-23; *Apollon*, p. 67.

Robert, Grace—The Borzoi Book of the Ballet. New York, Alfred A. Knopf, 1946.
Contents include: Notes on the following Stravinsky works. *Apollon Musagètes*, pp. 27-33; *Le Baiser de la Fée*, 38-41; *Les Noces*, pp. 201-204; *Petrouchka*, pp. 222-231; *Le Sacre du Printemps*, pp. 259-263.

Rosenfeld, Paul—By Way of Art: Criticisms of music, literature, painting, sculpture and dance. New York, Coward-McCann, 1928.
Contents include: *Renard.—Les Noces.*—We question Stravinsky.—Igor, tu n'est qu'un villain.

Rosenfeld, Paul—Discoveries of a Music Critic. New York, Harcourt, Brace & Co., 1936.
Contents include: Evolution of Stravinsky, pp. 170-196.

Rosenfeld, Paul—Musical Chronicle (1917–1923). New York, Harcourt, Brace & Co., 1923.
Contents include: The Stravinsky *Concertino*, pp. 97-104.

Rosenfeld, Paul—Musical Portraits. New York, Harcourt, Brace & Howe, 1920.
Contents include: Stravinsky, pp. 191-204.

Sabaneev, Leonid—Modern Russian Composers. Translated from the Russian by J. A. Joffe. New York, International Publishers, 1927.
Contents include: Igor Stravinsky, pp. 64-86.

Salazar, Adolfo—Music in Our Time: Trends in music since the romantic era. New York, W. W. Norton, 1946.
Contents include: Igor Stravinsky, pp. 277-296.

Saminsky, Lazare—Music of Our Day. New York, T. Y. Crowell, 1932.
Contents include: Scriabin and Stravinsky in review, pp. 189-193.

Scholes, Percy A.—Crotchets: A few short musical notes. New York, Oxford University Press, 1924.
Contents include: Some views on Stravinsky, pp. 144-161.

Scholes, Percy A.—Everyman and His Music. London, K. Paul, Trench & Trubner, 1917.
Contents include: Stravinsky, pp. 150-156.

Spaeth, Sigmund—A Guide to Great Orchestral Music. New York, The Modern Library, 1943.
Contents include: Igor Stravinsky, pp. 365-372.

Thomas, Henry & D. L.—Forty Famous Composers. New York, Halcyon House, 1948.
Contents include: Stravinsky, pp. 400-408.

Thomas, Henry & D. L.—Living Biographies of Great Composers. New York, Blue Ribbon Books, 1946.
Contents include: Igor Stravinsky, pp. 317-326.

Thomson, Virgil—The Art of Judging Music. New York, Alfred A. Knopf, 1948.
Contents include: *Le Sacre du Printemps* (performed by Boston Symphony, conducted by Bernstein), pp. 23-24.—*Oedipus Rex* (New York City Symphony, with Robert Shaw chorus, Bernstein conducting), pp. 179-181.—Stravinsky and New York Philharmonic, pp. 181-183.

Turner, W. J.—Music and Life. London, Methuen & Co., 1921.
   Contents include: Stravinsky, pp. 132-139.

Turner, W. J.—Musical Meanderings, by W. J. Turner. London, Methuen & Co., 1928.
   Contents include: Stravinsky's Soldier.—*Les Noces.*

Upton, George P. & Borowski, Felix—The Standard Concert Guide. New and revised edition. New York, Halcyon House, 1947.
   Contents include: Stravinsky, pp. 408-416.

Van Vechten, Carl—Music After the Great War, and Other Studies. New York, G. Schirmer, 1915.
   Contents include: Igor Stravinsky—a new composer, pp. 85-117.

Veinus, Abraham—Victor Book of Concertos. New York, Simon & Schuster, 1948.
   Contents include: Igor Stravinsky: *Capriccio,* pp. 390-393.

Von neuer Musik; Beitrage zur Erkentniss der neuezeitlichen Tonkunst. Köln am Rhein, F. J. Marcan, 1925.
   Contents include: Igor Stravinsky, by Boris de Schloezer, pp. 124-140.— Versuch einer Bibliographie über Strawinsky, by Wilhelm Altmann, pp. 311-314.

REFERENCES TO STRAVINSKY IN
PERIODICALS

Ansermet, Ernest—L'Oeuvre d'Igor Strawinsky. *In* La Revue Musicale. Année 2, no. 9, pp. 1-27. Paris, July 1921.

Ansermet, Ernest—Einführung in das Schaffen Igor Strawinskijs. *In* Musikblätter des Anbruch. Jahrg. 4, pp. 169-172. Wien, June 1922.

Ansermet, Ernest—Introduction de l'Oeuvre d'Igor Strawinsky. *In* Revue Pleyel. No. 18, pp. 15-20. Paris, March 1925.

Ansermet, Ernest—Introduccion a la Obra de Igor Strawinsky. *In* Nosotros. Ano 18, tomo 48, pp. 176-184. Buenos Aires, Oct. 1924.

Ansermet, Ernest—The Man and His Work: His First String Quartet. *In* Musical Courier. Vol. 71, no. 21, p. 41. Port. New York, Nov. 1915.

Asaf'ev, Boris—Uber die Art des Einflusses Strawinskys auf die zeitgenössische Musik. *In* Der Auftakt. Jahrg. 9, pp. 106-108. Prague, 1929.

Asaf'ev, Boris—Prozess der Formbildung bei Strawinsky. *In* Der Auftakt. Jahrg. 9, pp. 101-106. Prague, 1929.

Auric, Georges—L'Apothéose d'Igor Strawinsky. *In* Annales Politiques et Littéraires. Année 90, p. 233. Paris, March 1928.

Babitz, Sol—Stravinsky's Symphony in C (1940). A short analysis and commentary. *In* Musical Quarterly. Vol. 27, pp. 20-25. Music. New York, Jan. 1941.

Bal y Gay, Jesus—Las Escenas de Ballet de Stravinsky. *In* Nuestra Musica. Pp. 199-209. Mexico, Oct. 1947.

Balzer, Jurgen—Strawinskys Memoirer. *In* Dansk Musiktidsskrift. Vol. 10, pp. 203-206, Oct. 1935; pp. 116-118, May 1936. Copenhagen.
Review of Chroniques de ma Vie.

Bartos, P. F.—Igor Strawinskij: O Hudebni Skladbe. *In* Tempo. No. 20, pp. 30-32. Prague, Oct. 1947.

Bauer, Marion—Composite Stravinsky. *In* Modern Music. Vol. 14, p. 38. New York, Nov. 1936.
Review of Merle Armitage's book on the composer.

Bauer, Marion—Igor Stravinsky. *In* The Musical Leader. Vol. 47, no. 12, p. 277. Chicago, March 20, 1924.

Bayfield, Stanley—Igor Stravinsky. *In* New Music Review. Vol. 24, pp. 396-398. New York, Oct. 1925.

Bayliss, Stanley—The Ideas of Igor Stravinsky. *In* The Choir. Vol. 32, no. 375, pp. 40-41. London, March 1941.

Bellver, Enrique—Strawinsky. *In* Conservatorio. No. 7, pp. 7-8. Illus. Habana, Sept. 1946.

Berger, Arthur—Igor Stravinsky. *In* Listen. Vol. 3, pp. 3-8. Illus. New York, August 1943.

Bertrand, Paul—Les Idées de M. Igor Strawinsky. *In* Le Ménestrel. Année 98: April 24, pp. 139-140; May 8, pp. 155-156; June 5, pp. 187-188; July 3, p. 220. Paris, 1936.

Bertrand, Paul—Les Idées de M. Igor Strawinsky sur le Disque et la Radio. *In* Le Ménestrel. Année 98, no. 5, pp. 33-34. Paris, Jan. 31, 1936.

Blitzstein, Marc—(Capriccio). *In* Modern Music. Vol. 8, p. 42. New York, Jan. 1931.
Note on the performance of this work by the Boston Symphony Orchestra with Sanromá at the piano.

Blitzstein, Marc—Phenomenon of Stravinsky. *In* Musical Quarterly. Vol. 21, pp. 330-347. Music. New York, July 1935.
A critical estimate of the composer on ideological and musical grounds.

Boulanger, Nadia—Strawinsky. *In* Lectures on Modern Music, delivered under the auspices of the Rice Institute lectureship in music. Pp. 178-195. Houston, Texas, April 1926.
An analysis of Stravinsky's methods and works.

Boys, Henry—Stravinsky. *In* The Monthly Musical Record. Vol. 64: Sept., pp. 152-154; Nov., pp. 195-197; Dec., pp. 226-228. London, 1934.

Brelet, Gisèle—La Poétique d'Igor Strawinsky. *In* La Revue Musicale. Année 22, pp. 131-135. Paris, April 1946.

Review of Stravinsky's Poétique Musicale.

Browne, Andrew J.—Aspects of Stravinsky's Work. *In* Music and Letters. Vol. 11, pp. 360-366. Music. London, Oct. 1930.

Calvocoressi, M. D.—A Russian Composer of Today. *In* Musical Times. Vol. 52, pp. 511-512. London, August 1911.
One of the earliest notices in English to appear on the composer.

Canby, Edward T.—Stravinsky. *In* Saturday Review of Literature. Vol. 29, p. 39. New York, Sept. 21, 1946.

Carter, Elliott—Stravinsky and Other Moderns in 1940. *In* Modern Music. Vol. 17, pp. 164-167. New York, March 1930.

Carter, Elliott—With the Dancers. *In* Modern Music. Vol. 14, pp. 237-239. New York, May 1937.
On the Stravinsky-Balanchine ballet festival at the Metropolitan Opera House.

Chanler, Theodore—Stravinsky's Apologia. *In* Modern Music. Vol. 20, pp. 17-22. New York, Nov. 1942.

Chennevière, R. D.—The Two Trends of Modern Music in Stravinsky's Works. *In* Musical Quarterly. Vol. 5, pp. 169-174. New York, April 1919.

Chop, Max—Strawinsky—Abend in der Staatsoper. *In* Signale für die musikalische Welt. Jahrg. 83, no. 24, pp. 1055-1057. Berlin, June 17, 1925.
Note on three works: *L'Histoire du Soldat, Pulcinella* and *Renard*.

Chronological Progress in Musical Art. *In* Etude. Vol. 44, pp. 559-560. Illus. Philadelphia, August 1926.
An interview with the composer.

Cimbro, Attilio—Igor Stravinsky. *In* Il Pianoforte. Anno 3, no. 3, pp. 81-87. Port. Torino, March 15, 1922.

Coeuroy, André—Picasso and Stravinsky. *In* Modern Music. Vol. 5, pp. 3-8. Illus. New York, Jan. 1928.
A comparative estimate: the author comments, "Rarely has it been possible to strike so perfect a parallel between two contemporary representatives of kindred arts as exists between Picasso and Stravinsky."

Coleman, Francis—A Talk with Igor Stravinsky. *In* Dance. Pp. 14, 30. New York, April 1945.

Il Concerto per pianoforte ed orchestra di I. Stravinschi. *In* Musica d'Oggi. Anno 7, no. 1, p. 12. Milan, Jan. 1925.

Copland, Aaron—Stravinsky and Hindemith Premieres. *In* Modern Music. Vol. 9, pp. 85-88. New York, Jan. 1932.
Comment on Stravinsky's *Violin Concerto.*

Curjel, Hans—Strawinsky oder die künsterliche Atmosphäre von Paris. *In* Melos. Jahrg. 8, no. 4, pp. 167-171. Berlin, April 1929.

Dahl, Ingolf—Stravinsky in 1946. *In* Modern Music. Vol. 23, pp. 159-165. Illus. New York, Summer 1946.

Denby, Edwin—With the Dancers. *In* Modern Music. Vol. 19, p. 275. New York, May 1942.
Note on the Stravinsky-Balanchine *Circus Polka*, created for Ringling Brothers' Circus.

The Dionysian Spirit which Vitalizes the Music of Igor Stravinsky. *In* Current Opinion. Vol. 57, no. 2, pp. 108-109. New York, Aug. 1914.

Doflein, Erich—Über Strawinsky. *In* Melos. Jahrg. 5, no. 4, pp. 158-160. Berlin, Jan. 1926.

Downes, Olin—Boston Takes Stravinsky Music Seriously. *In* Musical Courier. Vol. 23, no. 6, p. 31. New York, Dec. 11, 1915.
Note on the Flonzaley Quartet performance of the composer's *Three Pieces for String Quartet*.

Druskin, M.—Das Klavier in Igor Strawinskys Kunst. *In* Der Auftakt. Jahrg. 9, no. 4, pp. 109-111. Prague, 1922.

Eaton, Quaintance—Stravinsky: Apostle of Today. *In* Musical America. Vol. 57, no. 1, p. 11. New York, Jan. 10, 1937.

Engel, Carl—Views and Reviews. *In* Musical Quarterly. Vol. 21, pp. 487-489. New York, Oct. 1935.
Review of the composer's Chroniques de ma Vie.

Ewen, David—The Decline of Stravinsky. *In* The Monthly Musical Record. Vol. 63, no. 750, pp. 179-180. London, Oct. 1933.

Ferroud, Pierre O.—Das Aesthetische Problem bei Strawinsky. *In* Melos. Vol. 9, pp. 365-370. Berlin, Aug. 1930.

Ferroud, Pierre O.—The Role of the Abstract in Igor Strawinsky's Work. *In* Chesterian. Vol. 11, no. 85, pp. 141-147. London, March 1930.

Fiechtner, Helmut—Igor Strawinsky: seine Persönlichkeit und Kunstauffassung. *In* Oesterreichissche Musikzeitschrift. Jahrg. 3, pp. 70-74. Wien, March 1948.

Finck, Henry T.—Igor Stravinsky. *In* The Mentor. Vol. 4, no. 18. Port. New York, 1916.
Brief biographical sketch.

Fleischer, Herbert—Rhythmische Veränderung durch Strawinsky. *In* Die Musik. Jahrg. 24, no. 9, pp. 654-657. Berlin, June 1932.

Fleischer, Herbert—Strawinsky. *In* Neue Rundschau. Jahrg. 43, pp. 862-863. Berlin, June 1932.

Fowlie, Wallace—Petrouchka's Wake. *In* Yale Romanic Studies. Vol. 22, pp. 249-253. New Haven, Conn., 1943.

Fox, Charles W.—Igor Strawinsky. *In* Music Library Association: Notes. Vol. 5, pp. 519-521. Washington, Sept. 1948.

Review of the newly published scores of *Orpheus* and *Concerto en Ré pour orchestre à cordes.*

Frankenstein, Alfred—Stravinsky in Beverly Hills. *In* Modern Music. Vol. 19, pp. 178-181. New York, March 1942.

Freitas e Castro, E.—Stravinsky no Brasil. *In* Boletino Latino-Americano de Musica. Año 4, no. 4, pp. 65-69. Montevideo, 1938.

Friedland, Martin—Igor Strawinskijs "Musikauffassung." *In* Allgemeine Musik-Zeitung. Jahrg. 58, no. 51, pp. 849-851. Berlin, Dec. 1931.

Fuller, Donald—Stravinsky—Full-length Portrait. *In* Modern Music. Vol. 23, pp. 45-46. New York, Winter 1946.
Note on concert by the New York Philharmonic conducted by the composer.

G., F.—La Théorique d'Igor Strawinsky. *In* Contrepoints. No. 3, pp. 12-30. Paris, March 1946.

G., H.—Stravinsky's Les Cinq Doigts. *In* The Musical Times. Vol. 63, p. 782. London, Nov. 1, 1922.
Note on this piano work.

Gair, Sidney R.—Notes on a Text by Strawinsky. *In* Sewanee Review. Vol. 55, no. 3, pp. 447-459. Sewanee, Tenn., July 1947.
An analysis of a statement made by the composer in his Harvard lecture series.

Gilman, Lawrence—From Stravinsky to Sibelius. *In* North American Review. Vol. 215, pp. 117-121. New York, Jan. 1922.

Gray, Cecil—Stravinsky. *In* The Nation and Athenaeum. Vol. 45, no. 23, pp. 734-735. London, Sept. 1929.
Review of Boris de Schloezer's book on Stravinsky.

Gutman, Hans—Puccini und Strawinsky. *In* Melos Zeitschrift für Musik. Jahrg. 2, no. 2, pp. 58-61. Mainz, Feb. 1942.

Gutman, Hans—Strawinsky, alt und neu; Uraufführung seines Violinkonzertes. *In* Der Auftakt. Jahrg. 11, no. 11, pp. 278-279. Prague, 1931.

Haggin, Bernard—Life and Work of Stravinsky. *In* The Nation. Vol. 143, pp. 494-495. New York, Oct. 1936.
Review of Merle Armitage's book on Stravinsky and Stravinsky's Chronicles of My Life.

Hell, Henri—L'Activité d'Igor Strawinsky. *In* La Revue Musicale. Année 22, no. 200, p. 188. Paris, May 1946.

Henry, Leigh—The Humour of Stravinsky. *In* The Musical Times. Vol. 60, pp. 670-673. Music. London, Dec. 1, 1919.

Henry, Leigh—Igor Stravinsky. *In* The Musical Times. Vol. 60, pp. 268-272. London, July 1, 1919.

Henry, Leigh—Igor Stravinsky and the Ballet. *In* The Musical News. Vol. 57, p. 4. London, July 5, 1919.

Henry, Leigh—Igor Stravinsky and the Objective Direction in Contemporary Music. *In* The Chesterian. No. 4, pp. 97-102. London, Jan. 1920.

Henry, Leigh—Stravinsky and the Pragmatic Criterion in Contemporary Music. *In* The English Review. Vol. 33, pp. 67-73. London, July 1921.

Heuss, Alfred—Igor Strawinsky im Gewandhaus. *In* Zeitschrift für Musik. Jahrg. 90, no. 19, pp. 19-23. Leipzig, Dec. 1923.

Hill, Edward B.—A Note on Stravinsky. *In* Harvard Musical Review. Vol. 2, no. 7, pp. 2-7. Boston, April 1914.
A brief estimate of his musical development.

Hill, Edward B.—Russian Nationalist Composers: Igor Stravinsky. *In* Etude. Vol. 59, pp. 815, 854. Port. Philadelphia, Dec. 1941.

Hoérée, Arthur—A propos du Strawinsky de Boris de Schloezer. *In* La Revue Musicale. Année 10, no. 11, pp. 153-161. Paris, Dec. 1929.
Review of Boris de Schloezer's book on Stravinsky.

Hull, Robert M.—The Wheel Comes Full Circle. *In* The Sackbut. Vol. 10, no. 4, pp. 100-102. London, Nov. 1929.
Note on the composer's evolution.

Hunt, Reginald—Stravinsky and Others. *In* Musical Opinion. Vol. 70, p. 253. London, May 1947.

Hussey, Dyneley—The Tragedy of Stravinsky. *In* The Dancing Times. Pp. 617-618. London, Sept. 1946.

Jacobi, Frederick, Jr.—Harvard Soirée. *In* Modern Music. Vol. 17, no. 1, pp. 47-48. New York, Oct. 1939.
Comment on Stravinsky's opening lecture at Harvard in the Charles E. Norton series.

Jacobi, Frederick—Stravinsky Begins his Chronicles. *In* Modern Music. Vol. 13, pp. 51-53. New York, Nov. 1935.
Comment on the composer's Chroniques de ma Vie, volume 1.

Jade, Ely—Igor Stravinski. *In* Franco-American Musical Society Quarterly Bulletin. Vol. 3, pp. 4-7. New York, 1924.
List of the composer's works with dates of first performances.

Kalisch, Alfred—Stravinsky Day by Day. *In* The Musical Times. Vol. 63, pp. 27-28. London, Jan. 1922.

Kall, Alexis—Stravinsky in the Chair of Poetry. *In* Musical Quarterly. Vol. 26, pp. 283-296. New York, July 1940.
On Stravinsky's lecture series at Harvard, 1939–40.

Kapp, Julius—Die Geschichte vom Soldaten, Pulcinella, Renard. *In* Blätter der Staatsoper. Jahrg. 5, no. 8, pp. 7-11. Berlin, June 1925.

Kirstein, Lincoln—Homage to Stravinsky. *In* Arts and Decoration. Vol. 46, pp. 14-15, 46. Illus. New York, May 1937.

Kolisch, Mitzi—Stravinsky—Russian of the Russians. *In* The Independent. Vol. 114, p. 559. Port. Boston, May 16, 1925.

Kozlenko, William—Sibelius and Stravinsky—An Appraisal. *In* Tempo. Vol. 1, no. 6, pp. 5-6. London, Aug. 1934.

Landormy, Paul—L'Art Russe et Igor Stravinsky. *In* Musique. Année 2, no. 9, pp. 933-939; no. 10, pp. 999-1003. Paris, June 1929.
Review of Boris de Schloezer's book on Stravinsky.

Lang, Paul H.—Stravinsky, the Enigma. *In* Saturday Review of Literature. Vol. 30, pp. 36-37. New York, May 3, 1947.

Leibowitz, René—Ein Brief aus Hollywood. *In* Stimmen. Jahrg. 1, no. 7, pp. 213-216. Berlin, 1948.
Schönberg and Stravinsky in California.

Leibowitz, René—Igor Strawinsky, ou le Choix de la Misère Musicale. *In* Le Temps Modern. Année 1, no. 7, pp. 1320-1336. Paris, April 1946.

Leibowitz, René—Schönberg and Stravinsky. *In* Partisan Review. Vol. 15, no. 3, pp. 361-365. New York, March 1948.
Schönberg and Stravinsky in California.

Levinson, André—Stravinsky and the Dance. *In* Theatre Arts Monthly. Vol. 8, pp. 741-754. New York, Nov. 1924.
A translation of the article in La Revue Musicale, Dec. 1923.

Lourié, Arthur—Le Capriccio de Strawinsky. *In* La Revue Musicale. Année 11, no. 103, pp. 353-355. Paris, April 1930.

Lourié, Arthur—Neo-gothic and Neo-classic. *In* Modern Music. Vol. 5, no. 3, pp. 3-8. New York, March 1928.
A comparative estimate of Schönberg and Stravinsky.

Lourié, Arthur—La Sonate pour Piano de Strawinsky. *In* La Revue Musicale. Année 6, no. 10, pp. 100-104. Paris, August 1925.

Lucas, V. N.—Musical Jottings: Stravinsky. *In* G. K.'s Weekly. Vol. 12, pp. 352-353. London, Feb. 7, 1931.

Maine, Basil—Stravinsky Again. *In* The Spectator. Vol. 146, pp. 180-181. London, Feb. 7, 1931.
Note on a Stravinsky concert by the BBC.

Maine, Basil—Stravinsky and Pure Music. *In* Musical Times. Vol. 63, no. 948, pp. 93-94. London, Feb. 1, 1922.

Malkiel, Henrietta—Modernists Have Ruined Modern Music, Says Stravinsky. *In* Musical America. Vol. 41, no. 18, p. 9. New York, Jan. 10, 1925.

Mangeot, A.—Chroniques de ma Vie de M. Igor Strawinsky. *In* Le Monde Musical. Année 47, no. 3, pp. 93-94. Paris, March 31, 1936.
Review of the composer's autobiography.

Mangeot, A.—Deux Festivals Igor Strawinsky. *In* Le Monde Musical. Année 39, no. 2, p. 59. Paris, Feb. 28, 1928.

Mantelli, Alberto—La Posizione di Strawinsky nella Musica Moderna. *In* La Rassegna Musicale. Anno 17, no. 1, pp. 44-52. Music. Rome, Jan. 1947.

Manuel, Roland—Concerto pour Piano, de Strawinsky. *In* Revue Pleyel. No. 10, pp. 27-28. Paris, July 1924.

Manuel, Roland—Strawinsky et la Critique. *In* Revue Pleyel. No. 9, pp. 17-18. Paris, June 1924.

Meltzer, Charles H.—Stravinsky—The Enigma. *In* The Forum. Vol. 66, pp. 241-248. New York, Sept. 1921.

Mendel, Arthur—Stravinsky. *In* The Nation. Vol. 132, pp. 279-280. New York, March 11, 1931.
Stravinsky compared with Elgar, Bloch and Loeffler.

Mersmann, Hans—Musiker der Zeit: Strawinsky. *In* Melos. Jahrg. 9, no. 2, pp. 529-531. Berlin, Dec. 1930.

Mila, Massimo—Europeismo di Stravinski. *In* Nuova Antologia. Anno 68, pp. 572-579. Rome, April 1933.

Mitchell, Edward—The Strawinsky Theories. *In* Musical Times. Vol. 63, no. 949, pp. 162-164. London, March 1922.
Stravinsky's music theories considered to be retrogressive and anti-intellectual.

Moore, Lillian—Stravinsky on Music for Ballet. *In* Dancing Times. Pp. 243-244. London, Feb. 1947.

Morris, R. O.—The Later Stravinsky. *In* The Nation. Vol. 27, no. 18, pp. 553-554. London, July 31, 1920.

Myers, Rollo H.—Some Thoughts Suggested by Strawinsky's Avertissement. *In* The Dominant. Vol. 1, no. 5, pp. 32-34. London, March 1928.
Comment on Stravinsky's statement on neo-classicism.

Nabokov, Nicolas—The Atonal Trail: A Communication. *In* Partisan Review. Vol. 15, no. 5, pp. 580-585. New York, May 1948.
Stravinsky's position as a composer defended against the criticism of Leibowitz.

Nabokov, Nicolas—Atonality and Obscurantism. *In* Partisan Review. Vol. 15, no. 10, pp. 1148-1151. New York, Oct. 1948.
Nabokov continues discussion with Leibowitz on Stravinsky.

Nabokov, Nicolas—Stravinsky, 1947. *In* Stimmen. Jahrg. 1, no. 1, pp. 6-12. Port. Berlin, Nov. 1947.

Nabokov, Nicolas—Stravinsky Now. *In* Partisan Review. Vol. 11, no. 3, pp. 324-334. New York, Summer 1944.

Notes of the Day: Stravinsky. *In* Monthly Musical Record. Vol. 62, no. 736, pp. 77-78. London, May 1932.
Review of André Schaeffner's book on the composer.

Osgood, H. O.—Stravinsky Conducts an Interview and a Concert. *In* Musical Courier. Vol. 90, no. 3, p. 7. New York, Jan. 15, 1925.

Oulmont, Charles—Besuch bei Strawinsky. *In* Melos. Jahrg. 14, no. 4, pp. 107-108. Port. Mainz, Feb. 1947.

Pannain, Guido—Igor Strawinsky. *In* La Rassegna Musicale. Anno 1, no. 5, pp. 281-296. Torino, May 1928.

Paoli, Domenico de—Igor Teodorovitch Strawinsky—Cenni Biografici. *In* Bollettino Bibliografico Musicale. Anno 2, no. 12, pp. 1-11. Milano, Dec. 1927.

Petit, Raymond—A Critical Portrait of Stravinsky. *In* Modern Music. Vol. 7, pp. 37-41. New York, April 1930.
Review of Boris de Schloezer's book on the composer.

Powell, Laurence—Strawinsky's Capriccio. *In* Disques, Vol. 1, no. 11, pp. 452-453. Philadelphia, Jan. 1931.

Pringsheim, Heinz—Aus Strawinskijs Falschmünserwerkstatt. *In* Allgemeine Musik-Zeitung. Jahrg. 51, p. 939. Berlin, Dec. 19, 1924.

Prunières, Henry—Igor Strawinsky: Chroniques de ma Vie. *In* La Revue Musicale. Année 17, pp. 239-240. Paris, March 1936.
Review of volume two of the composer's autobiography.

Ramuz, C. F.—Erinnerungen an Igor Strawinsky. *In* Schweizerische Musik-zeitung. Vol. 69, pp. 1-8. Zurich, Jan. 1, 1929.

Ramuz, C. F.—Oeuvres Complètes . . . Lausanne, H. L. Mermod, 1940–1941. 20 vols.
Contents include: Vol. 9, *L'Histoire du Soldat.* (Libretto.) Vol. 14, Souvenirs sur Igor Strawinsky.

Rhodes, Russell—American Ballet's All-Stravinsky Programme at the Metropolitan. *In* Dancing Times. Pp. 319-321. Illus. London, Jan. 1937.

Rosenfeld, Paul—A Stravinsky World Premiere. *In* The New Republic. Vol. 91, p. 18. New York, May 12, 1937.
Note on the Stravinsky-Balanchine festival at the Metropolitan.

Rosenfeld, Paul—European Music in Decay. *In* Scribner's Magazine. Vol. 89, no. 3, pp. 277-283. New York, March 1931.

Rosenfeld, Paul—Stravinsky. *In* The New Republic. Vol. 22, pp. 207-210. New York, April 14, 1920.
An estimate of the composer.

Rosenfeld, Paul—Stravinsky. *In* The New Republic. Vol. 70, pp. 128-129. New York, March 16, 1932.
Comment on the composer's recent lack of assurance.

Sabaneev, Leonid—The Stravinsky Legends. *In* The Musical Times. Vol. 69, pp. 785-787. London, Sept. 1, 1928.

Salvat, J.—Strawinsky at Barcelona. *In* Revista Musical Catalana. Ano 21, no. 224, pp. 85-87. Barcelona, April 1924.

Saminsky, Lazare—Mediterranean Stravinsky, a New Myth. *In* Modern Music. Vol. 9, pp. 137-138. New York, March 1932.
Comment on Domenico de Paoli's book on the composer.

Sanborn, Pitts—Koussevitzky and Stravinsky. *In* The Nation. Vol. 120, pp. 298-299. New York, March 18, 1925.
    Comparison of Koussevitzky and Stravinsky as interpreters of the composer's works.
Sanborn, Pitts—Stravinsky. *In* The Independent. Vol. 112, p. 212. Boston, April 12, 1924.
    The writer comments on Stravinsky's acceptance as an established composer.
Schaeffner, André—Le "Purisme" d'Igor Strawinsky. *In* Europe—Revue Mensuelle. Année 44, no. 174, pp. 184-202. Paris, June 1937.
Schaeffner, André—On Stravinsky, Early and Late. *In* Modern Music. Vol. 12, pp. 2-7. Port. New York, Nov. 1934.
Schaeffner, André—Stravinsky's Capriccio. *In* Modern Music. Vol. 7, pp. 31-34. New York, Feb. 1930.
    Note on a performance in Paris.
Schaeffner, André—Stravinsky's Two-Piano Concerto. *In* Modern Music. Vol. 13, pp. 35-36. New York, May 1936.
    Note on the Paris premiere of this work as performed by the composer and his son Soulima.
Scherber, Ferdinand—Ein Interview oder Igor Strawinsky's Kritik an der Kritik. *In* Signale für die musikalische Welt. Jahrg. 87, no. 13, pp. 408-409. Leipzig, March 27, 1929.
Schloezer, Boris de—A propos de la Sonate de Strawinsky. *In* Revue Pleyel. No. 26, pp. 18-20. Paris, Nov. 1925.
Schloezer, Boris de—L'Enigma di Stravinsky. *In* La Rassegna Musicale. Anno 7, no. 2, pp. 89-96. Torino, March 1934.
    An Italian version of the Modern Music article of Nov. 1932.
Schloezer, Boris de—The Enigma of Stravinsky. *In* Modern Music. Vol. 10, no. 1, pp. 10-17. New York, Nov. 1932.
Schloezer, Boris de—Igor Stravinsky. *In* The Dial. Vol. 85, no. 4, pp. 271-283, Oct. 1928; Vol. 86, no. 2, pp. 105-115, Feb. 1929; Vol. 86, no. 4, pp. 298-303, April 1929; Vol. 86, no. 6, pp. 463-474, June, 1929.
    A definitive estimate of the composer. Translated by Ezra Pound.
Schloezer, Boris de—Igor Stravinsky: Le Russe et L'Européen. *In* Bibliothèque Universelle et Revue de Genève. Pp. 38-52. Geneva, Jan. 1929.
Schloezer, Boris de—Igor Strawinsky, Serge Prokofieff. *In* Melos. Jahrg. 4, no. 10, pp. 469-481. Berlin, May 1925.
Schloezer, Boris de—Sur Stravinsky. *In* La Revue Musicale. Année 10, no. 4, pp. 1-19. Paris, Feb. 1929.
Schmidt-Garre, Helmut—Igor Strawinsky. *In* Neue Musik Zeitschrift. Jahrg. 2, no. 2, pp. 38-46. Port. Munich, Feb. 1948.

Schön, Ernst—A Stravinsky Festival at Frankfort-on-Main. *In* The Chesterian. Vol. 7, no. 52, pp. 127-128. London, Jan. 1926.
Concert conducted by the composer.

Schön, Ernst—Ueber Strawinskys Einfluss. *In* Melos. Jahrg. 8, no. 4, pp. 162-166. Berlin, April 1929.

Schönewolf, Karl—Gespräch mit Strawinski. *In* Die Musik. Jahrg. 21, no. 7, pp. 499-503. Berlin, April 1929.

Schulhoff, Erwin—Paraphäse über Hernn Strawinsky. *In* Der Auftakt. Jahrg. 4, no. 10, pp. 281-283. Prague, 1924.

Seltsam, W. H.—The Ballets of Igor Strawinski. *In* Phonograph Monthly Review. Vol. 4, no. 12, pp. 402-403. Boston, Sept. 1930.

Silber, Sidney—The Stravinsky Concerto. *In* The Music News. Vol. 21, no. 30, p. 25. Chicago, July 26, 1929.
An estimate of the *Piano Concerto*.

Slonimsky, Nicolas—Centenario de Strawinsky, Neuva York, Junio de 1982; Fiel y verdadera anticpacion del dia on que el maquinismo glorifique la musica. *In* Musicalia. Anno 4, no. 15, pp. 3-8. Havana, Jan. 1931.

Slonimsky, Nicolas—Centenari de Strawinsky, Nova York, Juny de 1982. *In* Revista Musical Catalana. Ano 28, no. 331, pp. 257-261. Barcelona, July 1931.

Smith, Moses—Stravinsky Meets the Boston Censor. *In* Modern Music. Vol. 21, pp. 171-173. New York, March 1944.
Note on a concert of the composer's later works conducted by himself.

Sound for Sound's Sake. *In* The Sackbut. Vol. 1, no. 4, pp. 153-156. London, Aug. 1920.
The writer comments, "Having nothing to say on any subjects of any importance, he announces that trivialities are greatly to be preferred."

Souvtchinsky, Pierre—Igor Strawinsky. *In* Contrepoints. No. 2, pp. 19-31. Paris, Feb. 1946.

Souvtchinsky, Pierre—Le Strawinsky d'Igor Glebov. *In* Musique. Année 3, no. 6, pp. 250-253. Paris, March 15, 1930.
Review of Glebov's book on the composer.

Stefan, Paul—Strawinsky, Zeit und Raum. *In* Anbruch Montsschrift für Moderne Musik. Jahrg. 14, no. 4, pp. 70-72. Wien, April 1932.

Steinhardt, Erich—Igor Strawinski. *In* Die Musik. Jahrg. 23, no. 6, pp. 574-577. Berlin, May 1931.

Stravinsky, Igor—Avant Le Sacre. *In* La Revue Musicale. Année 16, pp. 1-14. Paris, Jan. 1935.
A section of the composer's Chroniques de ma Vie.

Stravinsky, Igor—Avertissement. *In* The Dominant. Vol. 1, no. 2, pp. 13-14. London, Dec. 1927.

The composer's statement on classicism and neoclassicism. Text in English and French.

Stravinsky, Igor—Early Musical Influence in My Life. *In* The Etude. Vol. 55, no. 3, pp. 155-156. Port. New York, March 1937.
An extract from his autobiography.

Strawinsky, Igor—Kilka Uwag ot zu Neoklasycyzmie. *In* Muzyka. Vol. 4, no. 12, pp. 565-566. Warsaw, Dec. 1927.
The composer's statement on neoclassicism.

Strawinsky, Igor—La Musica en las Peliculas. *In* Conservatorio. No. 8, p. 11. Habana, Oct. 1947.

Strawinski, Igor—O mych Ostatnich Utworach. *In* Muzyka. Vol. 1, no. 1, pp. 15-17. Warsaw, Nov. 1924.
Stravinsky's statement on his own later works.

Stravinsky, Igor—Some Ideas about my Octuor. *In* The Arts. Vol. 5, no. 1, pp. 5-6. New York, Jan. 1924.
"The aim I sought in this *Octuor*, which is also the aim I sought with the greatest energy in all my recent works, is to realize a musical composition through means which are emotive in themselves."

Stravinsky, Igor—Stravinsky et Tchaikovsky. *In* La Revue Musicale. Année 3, no. 9, pp. 87-88. Paris, July 1922.
A letter by Stravinsky in defense of Tchaikovsky.

Stravinsky, Igor—Stravinsky Previsions a New Music. *In* Current Opinion. Vol. 78, pp. 329-330. New York, March 1925.
A statement by the composer on music in general and the merits of the player-piano. He comments, "There is a new polyphonic truth in the player-piano."

Stravinsky, Igor—Ueber den Vortrag. *In* Melos. Jahrg. 14, no. 1, pp. 6-8. Port. Mainz, Nov. 1946.

Stravinsky, Igor—Why People Dislike My Music. *In* Musical Forecast. Vol. 17, no. 6, pp. 1, 12. Pittsburgh, Feb. 1930.

Igor Stravinsky, Ragtime. *In* The Chesterian. No. 7, p. 215. London, May 1920.
Note on performance at Aeolian Hall, London, conducted by Sir Arthur Bliss.

Igor Stravinsky, sua Visita a Mexico. *In* Boletino de la Orquesta Sinfonica de Mexico. No. 4, pp. 63-65. Mexico, 1940.

Strawinsky—Aufregung. Stimmen aus dem Publikum. *In* Der Auftakt. Jahrg. 4, no. 10, pp. 307-312. Prague, 1925.

Stravinsky, the Extremist. *In* The British Musician. Vol. 10, no. 8, pp. 181-182. London, August 1934.

Stravinsky's Strange New "Sniffs and Snorts." *In* Current Opinion. Vol. 69, no. 4, pp. 491-492. New York, Oct. 1920.

Extracts from reviews of the London critics.

Straus, Henrietta—On the Giving of Stravinsky. *In* The Nation. Vol. 118, p. 512. New York, April 30, 1924.
About the various conductors' interpretations of Stravinsky's works.

Strobel, Heinrich—Strawinsky Privat. *In* Melos. Jahrg. 10, no. 10, pp. 315-318. Berlin, Oct. 1931.

Strobel, Heinrich—Strawinskys Violinkonzert. *In* Melos. Jahrg. 10, no. 11, pp. 377-379. Berlin, Oct. 1931.

Strobel, Heinrich—Strawinskys Weg. *In* Melos. Jahrg. 8, no. 4, pp. 158-162. Berlin, April 1929.

Strobel, Heinrich—Vom Apollon zur Psalmensinfonie. *In* Melos. Jahrg. 10, no. 7, pp. 219-224. Berlin, July 1931.

Stuckenschmidt, H. H.—Strawinsky oder die Vereinigung des Univerein-baren. *In* Musikblätter des Anbruch. Jahrg. 14, no. 4, pp. 67-70. Wien, April 1932.

Tangeman, Robert—Stravinsky's Two-Piano Works. *In* Modern Music. Vol. 22, pp. 93-98. New York, Jan. 1945.

Tansman, Alexandre—Les Ballets de Strawinsky: en concordance avec son évolution musicale. *In* Archives Internationales de la Danse. No. 1, pp. 15-16. Paris, Jan. 1933.

Tappolet, Willy—Strawinsky am Genfersee. *In* Melos. Jahrg. 8, no. 4, pp. 172-174. Berlin, April 1929.

Thomas, Juan M.—Un Musicien Méditeranéen. (Strawinsky.) *In* Musique. Année 1, no. 11, pp. 485-487. Paris, Sept. 15, 1928.

Thomson, Virgil—In the Theatre. *In* Modern Music. Vol. 14, pp. 236-237. New York, May 1937.
On the Stravinsky-Balanchine festival at the Metropolitan Opera House.

Thomson, Virgil—The Official Stravinsky. *In* Modern Music. Vol. 13, pp. 57-58. New York, May 1936.
Review of volume two of the composer's Chroniques de ma Vie.

Thompson, Oscar—New Stravinsky Ballet Achieves World Premiere. *In* Musical America. Vol. 57, no. 9, pp. 19-20. Illus. New York, May 10, 1937.
On the Stravinsky-Balanchine festival at the Metropolitan Opera House.

Tiby, Ottario—Igor Strawinsky. *In* Il Pianoforte. Anno 5, no. 8, p. 216. Torino, Aug. 1924.

Tschuppik, Walter—Gespräch mit Strawinsky. *In* Der Auftakt. Jahrg. 4, no. 10, pp. 280-281. Prague, 1924.

Turner, W. J.—Schönberg and Stravinsky. *In* New Statesman and Nation. Vol. 2, no. 39, p. 642. London, Nov. 21, 1931.

Turner, W. J.—Stravinsky and Goossens. *In* The New Statesman. Vol. 33, no. 844, p. 370. London, July 29, 1929.

Concert conducted by Goossens with the composer at the piano in his *Piano Concerto.*

Van Vechten, Carl—A New Principle in Music: Stravinsky and his work. *In* The Russian Review. Vol. 1, no. 3, pp. 160-164. New York, April 1916. An estimate of the composer's music.

Verbitsky, Bernardo—Algo sobre Strawinsky. *In* Nosotros. Ano 2, pp. 180-190. Buenos Aires, Oct. 1937.

Vermeulen, Matthijs—Rondom Stravinsky. *In* Die Muziek. Jaarg. 2, no. 1, pp. 1-12. Illus. Amsterdam, 1927.

Vuillermoz, Emile—Igor Strawinsky. *In* S. I. M., La Revue Musicale. Année 8, no. 5, pp. 15-21. Illus., music. Paris, May 1912.

Watkins, Mary F.—Who's Who Among Ballet Composers. *In* Dance Magazine. Vol. 12, no. 1, pp. 17, 47. Illus. New York, May 1929. Note on Stravinsky and the Diaghilev Ballet.

Weissmann, Adolf—Igor Strawinsky. *In* Blätter der Staatsoper. Jahrg. 5, no. 8, pp. 1-6. Berlin, June 1925.

Weissmann, Adolf—The Influence of Schönberg and Stravinsky in Germany. *In* The Music Bulletin. Vol. 9, no. 2, pp. 45-51. London, Feb. 1927.

Weissmann, Adolf—Strawinsky. *In* Musikblätter des Anbruch. Jahrg. 6, pp. 228-234. Wien, June 1924.

Weissmann, Adolf—Strawinsky spielt sein Klavierkonzert. *In* Musikblätter des Anbruch. Jahrg. 6, no. 10, pp. 407-409. Berlin, Nov. 1924.

Wellesz, Egon—Strawinsky. *In* Der Auftakt. Jahrg. 2, no. 2, pp. 39-41. Prague, 1922.

Westrheene, P. A. van—Strawinsky. *In* Caecilia en het Muziekcollege. Vol. 82, no. 13, pp. 203-205. Amsterdam, June 10, 1925.

Weterings, J.—Au Sujet de Stravinsky. *In* La Revue Musicale Belge. Année 6, no. 14, pp. 1-2. Brussells, July 20, 1930.

Weterings, J.—Stravinsky. *In* La Revue Musicale Belge. Année 3, no. 18, pp. 1-4. Brussells, Sept. 20, 1927.

Wiborg, Mary H.—Igor Stravinsky, One of the Great Russians. *In* Arts and Decoration. Vol. 22, no. 3, p. 36. Port. New York, Jan. 1925.

Wilson, Edmund—Stravinsky. *In* New Republic. Vol. 42, pp. 156-157. New York, April 1, 1925. Comment on the composer's *Octuor*, *Violin Concerto* and other recent works.

Wise, C. Stanley—Impressions of Igor Strawinsky. *In* Musical Quarterly. Vol. 2, no. 2, pp. 248-256. Port. New York, April 1916.

Wyatt, Euphemia V.—Notes on Ballet. *In* Catholic World. Vol. 145, no. 867, pp. 340-342. New York, June 1937.

Note on the Stravinsky-Balanchine festival at the Metropolitan Opera House.

REFERENCES TO SPECIFIC WORKS
BY STRAVINSKY

APOLLON MUSAGETES

Denby, Edwin—With the Dancers. *In* Modern Music. Vol. 15, pp. 184-185. New York, March 1938.
Apollo at the Metropolitan.

Gutman, Hans—Strawinsky: Apollon Musagètes. *In* Der Auftakt. Jahrg. 8, no. 9, pp. 224-225. Prague, 1928.

Henry, Leigh—Stravinsky Rounds off a Circle. *In* Musical America. Vol. 40, no. 14, pp. 7, 16. New York, July 21, 1928.
Note on London production of *Apollon.*

Jacobi, Frederick—The New Apollo. *In* Modern Music. Vol. 5, pp. 11-15. New York, May 1928.
An appraisal of Stravinsky's *Apollon Musagètes.*

Klingsor, Tristan—Ballets Russes: Apollon, d'Igor Strawinsky. *In* Le Monde Musical. Année 39, no. 6, p. 218. Paris, June 30, 1928.
Note on Paris production of this work.

Lederman, Minna—With the Dancers. *In* Modern Music. Vol. 23, p. 71. New York, Winter 1946.
Note on Balanchine's *Apollon.*

Lourié, Arthur—A propos de l'Apollon d'Igor Strawinsky. *In* Musique. Année 1, no. 3, pp. 117-119. Paris, Dec. 15, 1928.

Lourié, Arthur—Stravinky's Apollo. *In* The Dominant. Vol. 1, no. 10, pp. 20-21. London, August 1928.

Prunières, Henry—Ballets Russes. *In* La Revue Musicale. Année 9, no. 9, pp. 287-288. Paris, July 1, 1928.
Critique of *Apollon.*

Redlich, Hans F.—Strawinsky's Apollon Musagètes. *In* Anbruch Monatschrift für Moderne Musik. Jahrg. 11, pp. 41-44. Berlin, Jan. 1929. Music.

Sabaneev, Leonid—Dawn or Dusk? Stravinsky's New Ballets, Apollo and The Fairy Kiss. *In* The Musical Times. Vol. 70, pp. 403-406. London, May 1929.

Schloezer, Boris de—Apollon Musagètes. *In* Musica d'Oggi. Anno 11, no. 1, pp. 8-12. Milan, Jan. 1929.

Schloezer, Boris de—Apollon Musagètes. *In* La Revista de Musica. Ano 2, no. 6, pp. 81-87. Buenos Aires, Dec. 15, 1928.

Seltsam, William—The Ballets of Igor Strawinski. *In* Phonograph Monthly
    Review. Vol. 5, no. 1, pp. 12-13. Boston, Oct. 1930.
    Special note on *Apollon*.
Turner, W. J.—Apollon Musagètes. *In* The New Statesman. Vol. 31, no.
    792, pp. 388-389. London, June 30, 1928.
    An estimate of this work.

LE BAISER DE LA FEE

Lederman, Minna—With the Dancers. *In* Modern Music. Vol. 23, pp. 137-
    138. New York, Spring 1946.
    On the Stravinsky-Balanchine ballet, *Baiser de la Fée*, as performed by
    the Ballet Russe de Monte Carlo.
Mangeot, A.—Les Ballets de Mme. Ida Rubinstein. *In* Le Monde Musical.
    Année 39, no. 12, p. 413. Paris, Dec. 1928.
    Review of the premiere.
Manuel, Roland—Le Baiser de la Fée. *In* Musique. Année 2, no. 3, pp. 657-
    659. Paris, Dec. 15, 1928.
Prunières, Henry—Les Ballets d'Ida Rubinstein à l'Opéra. *In* La Revue Musi-
    cale. Année 10, p. 243. Paris, Jan. 1, 1929.
    Comment on production of *Le Baiser de la Fée*.
Prunières, Henry—Stravinsky and Ravel. *In* Modern Music. Vol. 6, pp. 35-39.
    New York, Winter 1928.
    Note on the composer's *Baiser de la Fée* as presented in Paris by Ida
    Rubinstein's company.
Stravinsky Ballet at Sadlers Wells. *In* The New Statesman and Nation. Vol.
    10, no. 249, pp. 812-813. London, Nov. 30, 1935.
    Note on production of *Baiser de la Fée*, with choreography by Fred-
    erick Ashton.

DANSES CONCERTANTES

Fuller, Donald—Society Notes in New York. *In* Modern Music. Vol. 20, pp.
    257-258. New York, May 1943.
    Note on a performance of *Danses Concertantes*.
Lederman, Minna—With the Dancers. *In* Modern Music. Vol. 22, pp. 60-61.
    New York, Nov. 1944.
    On the ballet *Danses Concertantes*.

L'HISTOIRE DU SOLDAT

Ansermet, Ernest—L'Histoire du Soldat. *In* The Chesterian. No. 10, pp. 289-
    293. London, Oct. 1920.

Meadmore, W. S.—Stravinsky's The Soldier's Tale. *In* Musical Standard. Vol. 30, no. 518, pp. 38-39. London, July 30, 1927.
> Comment on the London production in which the writer says, "I refuse to take *The Tale of the Soldier* seriously. It is not even amusing, one can only smile at the absurdity of the libretto . . ."

Mila, Massimo—L'Histoire du Soldat, di Stravinsky e Ramuz. *In* Nuova Antologia. Anno 70, pp. 471-472. Rome, Feb. 1935.

Ramuz, C. F.—De Geschiednis van den Soldat. Gelezen, gespeeld, gedanst. In twee deelen. Tekst van C. F. Ramuz, muziek van Igor Strawinsky. *In* Gids. Jaarg. 90, no. 4, pp. 165-185. Amsterdam, 1926.

Ramuz, C. F.—L'Histoire du soldat (parlée, jouée, dansée). Lausanne, Mermod, 1944. 60 pp.
> Libretto. French text.

Ramuz, C. F.—The Soldier's Tale, to be read, played and danced. In two parts. English version by Rosa Newmarch. London, J. & W. Chester, 1924. 32 pp.
> Libretto of this work.

Schnoor, Hans—Strawinskys Geschichte vom Soldaten. *In* Der Auftakt. Jahrg. 4, no. 10, pp. 276-280. Prague, 1924.

Sonenfield, Irwin—Juilliard Goes Modern with a Vengeance. *In* The Musician. Vol. 53, p. 43. Philadelphia, June 1948.
> Note on production of *The Soldier's Tale.*

Tornblom, Folke H.—Stravinskijs Historien om en Soldat. *In* Musik-varlden. Vol. 1, no. 3, pp. 11-13. Illus. Stockholm, April 1945.

Turner, W. J.—Stravinsky in London and Paris. *In* The New Statesman. Vol. 15, no. 381, pp. 474-475. London, July 31, 1920.
> Note on *L'Histoire* and other works performed in Paris.

Turner, W. J.—Stravinsky's Soldier. *In* The New Statesman. Vol. 29, no. 742, pp. 445-446. London, July 16, 1927.
> Critique of London performance of *L'Histoire du Soldat.*

JEU DE CARTES

The Card Party by Stravinsky. *In* Cue. Vol. 5, no. 26, p. 9. Illus. New York, April 24, 1937.

Denby, Edwin—With the Dancers. *In* Modern Music. Vol. 18, no. 1, pp. 61-63. New York, Nov. 1940.
> Note on the ballet *The Card Party* as presented by the Monte Carlo Company.

Kirstein, Lincoln—Working with Stravinsky. *In* Modern Music. Vol. 14, pp. 143-146. New York, March 1937.
> On the collaboration for the ballet *Jeu de Cartes.*

Pfauter, Karl–Strawinsky's Kartenspiel. *In* Der Tanz. Jahrg. 10, no. 12, pp. 24-25. Berlin, Dec. 1937.

MAVRA

Jacobi, Frederick–Reflections on Ariadne and Mavra. *In* Modern Music. Vol. 12, pp. 75-78. New York, Jan. 1935.
Note on *Mavra* as performed by the Philadelphia Orchestra under the direction of Alexander Smallens.

Mangeot, A.–Ballets Russes. *In* Le Monde Musical. Année 33, pp. 215-216. Paris, June 1922.
Note on performance of *Mavra* and *Renard*.

Mavra Reveals New Stravinsky to Paris. *In* Musical America. Vol. 36, no. 10, p. 10. New York, July 1, 1922.

Milhaud, Darius–Strawinskys neue Bühnenwerke. *In* Musikblätter des Anbruch. Jahrg. 4, no. 17, pp. 260-262. Wien, Nov. 1922.
Note on Paris productions of *Mavra* and *Renard*.

Thompson, Oscar–Stravinsky's Mavra is Introduced to Philadelphia. *In* Musical America. Vol. 55, no. 1, pp. 3, 7. New York, Jan. 10, 1935.

LES NOCES

Adler, Lawrence. Epilogue of the Season. *In* The Nation. Vol. 128, p. 568. New York, May 8, 1929.
Note on the ballet *Les Noces*.

Belaiev, Victor–Les Noces, an Outline. Translated from the Russian by S. W. Pring. London, Oxford University Press, 1928. 37 pp. Illus., music.
An analysis of the form, harmony, rhythm and themes of this work.

Casella, Alfredo–Stravinsky's Noces Villageoises. *In* Arts. Vol. 9, no. 2, pp. 73-75. Illus. New York, Feb. 1926.

Castelnuovo-Tedesco, Mario–Leggendo Les Noces di Strawinski. *In* Il Pianoforte. Anno 8, no. 1, pp. 15-25. Torino, Jan. 1927.

Chanler, Margaret– Memory Makes Music. New York, Stephen-Paul, 1948.
Contents include: Comments on the original production of *Les Noces*, and other performances of Stravinsky's ballets in Paris, 1923.

Denby, Edwin–Revival of Diaghilev's Noces. *In* Modern Music. Vol. 13, pp. 44-46. New York, May 1936.
Comment on the ballet as produced by the Monte Carlo Ballet.

Desderi, E.–Igor Strawinsky, Les Noces. *In* Rivista Musicale Italiana. Vol. 34, pp. 464-466. Torino, Dec. 1927.

Glassgold, C. A.–A New Production of Les Noces. *In* Arts. Vol. 15, no. 5, pp. 347-348. New York, May 1929.

Gray, Cecil—The Music of Les Noces. *In* Nation and Athenaeum. Vol. 39, no. 14, p. 416. London, July 10, 1926.

Hammond, Richard—Viewing Les Noces in 1929. *In* Modern Music. Vol. 6, pp. 19-25. New York, March 1929.

Manuel, Roland—Igor Stravinsky's Les Noces. *In* The Chesterian. No. 33, pp. 1-4. London, Sept. 1923.

Opdyke, Mary E.—Stravinsky's New Black and White Ballet, Les Noces. *In* Musical Courier. Vol. 87, no. 1, p. 27. Illus. New York, July 5, 1923.
Review of the Paris production at the Gaîté-Lyrique.

Program of Les Noces. For the League of Composers' stage premiere, under the direction of Leopold Stokowski . . . at the Metropolitan Opera House . . . April 25, 1929. 12 pp. Illus.
Program contains scenario of *Les Noces*.

Schaeffner, André—Ballets Russes: Noces d'Igor Strawinsky. *In* Le Ménestrel. Année 85, no. 26, pp. 287-288. Paris, June 29, 1923.
Note on performance at the Gaîté-Lyrique, Paris.

Stokowski, Leopold—Concerning Stravinsky's Les Noces. *In* Musical Courier. Vol. 98, no. 16, pp. 24. Philadelphia, April 20, 1929.

Stravinski, Igor—Prima Esecuzione in Italia della Cantata Ballo, Le Nozze, di Igor Strawinski. Milano, Unione Tipografia, 1927. 48 pp.
Libretto of *Les Noces*, Italian text.

Turner, W. J.—The Latest Musical Masterpiece. *In* New Statesman. Vol. 27, no. 687, pp. 293-294. London, June 26, 1926.
Note on the Diaghilev production of *Les Noces*.

Vuillermoz, Emile—Chroniques et Notes. Noces. *In* La Revue Musicale. Année 4, no. 10, pp. 69-72. Paris, Aug. 1923.

Wilson, Edmund—Stravinsky and Others. *In* New Republic. Vol. 46, pp. 73-74. New York, March 10, 1926.
Comment on *Les Noces*.

Wortham, H. E.—Music for the Month. *In* Apollo. Vol. 4, no. 20, pp. 88-89. London, August 1926.
Includes comment by H. G. Wells on his enthusiasm for *Les Noces*.

OEDIPUS REX

Bonner, Eugene—The Oedipus Rex of Stravinsky. *In* The Outlook. Vol. 148, no. 13, p. 504. New York, March 28, 1928.
Note on the New York premiere of this work conducted by Serge Koussevitzky, with the Harvard Glee Club.

Burke, Kenneth—Musical Chronicle. *In* The Dial. Vol. 84, pp. 445-447. New York, May 1928.
An estimate of Stravinsky's *Oedipus Rex*.

Coeuroy, André—Oedipus and Other Music Heard in Paris. *In* Modern Music. Vol. 5, pp. 39-42. New York, Nov. 1927.

Copland, Aaron—Stravinsky's Oedipus Rex. *In* The New Republic. Vol. 54, pp. 68-69. New York, Feb. 29, 1928.

Edipo Re di I. Strawinski. *In* Musica d'Oggi. Anno 9, no. 10, pp. 284-286. Milano, Oct. 1927.

Epstein, Peter—Opera-oratorio—zur Gegenwartslage der Oper. *In* Die Musik. Jahrg. 20, no. 12, pp. 866-872. Berlin, Sept. 1928.
Discussion of the opera-oratorio form with note on Stravinsky's *Oedipus Rex*.

Ficker, Rudolf—Stimmen zum Oedipus Rex. *In* Neue Musikzeitung. Jahrg. 49, Heft 16, p. 513. Stuttgart, May 1928.

Gilbert, Richard—Oedipus Rex and Pas d'Acier. *In* Arts. Vol. 17, pp. 640-641. New York, June 1931.

Henry, Leigh—Oedipus Rex and the Objective Music Drama. *In* Musical Courier. Vol. 103, pp. 7, 10. Illus. New York, Aug. 1, 1931.

Kernochan, Marshall—Oedipus Rex. *In* The Outlook. Vol. 158, no. 2, p. 60. New York, May 13, 1931.
On performance at the Metropolitan by the League of Composers.

Program of Oedipus Rex for the League of Composers' stage premiere. Directed by Leopold Stokowski . . . New York, April 1931. 16 pp. illus.
Program contains scenario of this work.

Lourié, Arthur—Oedipus Rex. *In* La Revue Musicale. Année 8, no. 8, pp. 240-253. Illus., music. Paris, June 1927.

Lourié, Arthur—Oedipus Rex. Opern-Oratorium nach Sophokles von Igor Strawinsky. *In* Blätter der Staatsoper. Jahrg. 8, no. 19, pp. 9-13. Berlin, Feb. 1928.

Lourié, Arthur—Oedipus Rex von Igor Strawinsky; deutsche Uebertragung aus dem Russischen von H. Rabeneck. Berlin, New York, Russischer Musikverlag, 1927. 13 pp.
Libretto, German text.

Mersmann, Hans—Strawinsky: Oedipus Rex, zur Frage der Antikeoper. *In* Melos. Jahrg. 7, no. 4, pp. 180-183. Berlin, April 1928.

Oedipus Rex. *In* Le Monde Musical. Année 38, no. 8, pp. 325-326. Paris, Sept. 30, 1927.
A review of the first performance of this work.

Rosenfeld, Paul—Oedipus Rex, Cocteau and Stravinsky. *In* The New Republic. Vol. 66, pp. 356-357. New York, May 13, 1931.

Sabaneev, Leonid—Russian Music at Paris: Stravinsky's Oedipus Rex. *In* The Musical Times, Vol. 68, pp. 749-750. London, August 1, 1927.

Sabaneev, Leonid—Stravinsky's Oedipus. *In* The Chesterian. Vol. 8, no. 64, pp. 258-261. London, July 1927.

Schloezer, Boris de—L'Oedipus Rex de Strawinsky. *In* La Revue Pleyel. No. 45, pp. 291-293. Paris, June 1927.

Sessions, Roger—On Oedipus Rex. *In* Modern Music. Vol. 5, pp. 9-15. New York, March 1928.

Stefan, Paul—Antinomie der neuen Oper: Kurt Weill und Strawinsky. *In* Musikblätter des Anbruch. Jahrg. 10, pp. 119-122. Illus. Wien, March 1928.
Note on *Oedipus Rex.*

Straus, Henrietta—Oedipus Rex. *In* The Nation. Vol. 126, pp. 387-388. New York, April 4, 1928.
Performance by Boston Symphony Orchestra with the Harvard Glee Club.

Strobel, Heinrich—Strawinsky's Neuklassizismus: Oedipus Rex. *In* Neue Musikzeitung. Jahrg. 49, pp. 433-437. Stuttgart, April 1928.

Turner, W. J.—Stravinsky and Hindemith. *In* The New Statesman and Nation. Vol. 11, no. 261, pp. 262-263. London, Feb. 1936.
Note on *Oedipus Rex* as performed by the BBC under the baton of Ansermet.

Weissmann, Adolf—Oper. *In* Die Musik. Jahrg. 20, no. 7, pp. 539-540. Berlin, April 1928.
Comment on *Oedipus Rex.*

L'OISEAU DE FEU

Applin, Arthur—The Stories of the Russian Ballet. New York, John Lane Co., 1911.
Contents include: *L'Oiseau de Feu*, pp. 79-82. Port.

Beaumont, Cyril W.—L'Oiseau de Feu, decorated by Ethelbert White. London, Beaumont, 1919. 16 pp.

Benois, Alexandre—Reminiscences of the Russian Ballet. London, Putnam, 1941.
Contents include: *L'Oiseau de Feu*, pp. 301-308.

Evans, Edwin—The Music of L'Oiseau de Feu. *In* Dancing Times. Pp. 400-401. Illus. London, July 1939.

Harrer, Joseph R.—Der Feuervogel—Paraphräse in Worten auf Stravinskys Musik. *In* Der Tanz. Jahrg. 11, no. 12. Berlin, Oct. 1929.

Matherly, Mildred—Fourth Graders Enjoy Stravinsky's Firebird Suite. *In* School Arts. Vol. 42, p. 288. Worcester, Mass., April 1943.

Nijinsky, Romola—Nijinsky, by His Wife. Foreword by Paul Claudel. New York, Simon & Schuster, 1934.
Contents include: Note on the first production of *L'Oiseau de Feu*, pp. 103-105.

Stokes, Adrian—Russian Ballets, by Adrian Stokes. Illustrated. New York, E. P. Dutton & Co., 1936.
Contents include: *Firebird*, pp. 113-124.

Vuillermoz, Emile—Musiques d'Aujourd'hui. Paris, Les Editions G. Cres, 1923.
Contents include: La réorchestration de *L'Oiseau de Feu*.

PERSÉPHONE

Chantavoine; Jean—Ballets de Mme Rubinstein: Perséphone de MM. André Gide et Strawinsky. *In* Le Ménestrel. Année 96, no. 19, pp. 178-179. Paris, May 11, 1934.

Cingria, C. A.—Perséphone et la Critique. *In* La Nouvelle Revue Française. Année 22, no. 251, pp. 297-301. Paris, August 1934.

Gide, André—Perséphone, Poema de André Gide y Musica de Igor Strawinsky . . . El poema en su idioma original y una version libre de Jorges Luis Borges. *In* Sur. Ano 6, no. 19, pp. 17-53. Buenos Aires, 1936.
French and Spanish text of the libretto.

Jacobi, Frederick—On Hearing Stravinsky's Perséphone. *In* Modern Music. Vol. 12, pp. 112-115. New York, March 1935.
Performance conducted by the composer with Boston Symphony Orchestra and Cecilia Chorus.

McN.—London Concerts. Perséphone. *In* The Musical Times. Vol. 76, p. 65. London, Jan. 1935.
Note on performance by the BBC.

Mangeot, A.—Les Ballets de Mme Ida Rubinstein. Perséphone. *In* Le Monde Musical. Année 45, no. 5, pp. 147-150. Paris, May 1934.
Note on first performance with a statement on the work by the composer.

Paoli, Domenico de—Neuc Werke von Malipiero und Strawinsky. *In* Schweizerische Musikzeitung. Jahrg. 73, no. 20, pp. 649-652. Zurich, Oct. 15, 1933.
Comment on *Perséphone*.

Prunières, Henry—Perséphone d'Igor Strawinsky aux Ballets de Mme Ida Rubinstein. *In* La Revue Musicale. Année 15, pp. 380-382. Paris, May 1934.
Comment on first performance. "The score is splendidly balanced, the choruses are superb, and some of them among the greatest things Strawinsky has ever given us . . ."

Rosenfeld, Paul—The Mystery of Perséphone. *In* The New Republic. Vol. 82, pp. 213-214. New York, April 3, 1935.

Schloezer, Boris de—Les Spectacles Ida Rubinstein. *In* La Nouvelle Revue Française. Année 22, no. 249, pp. 1027-1030. Paris, June 1934.
Critique of the work *Perséphone*.

Schloezer, Boris de—(Perséphone). *In* La Nouvelle Revue Française. Année 22, no. 251, pp. 301-303. Paris, August 1934.
Reply to A. Cingria's statement on *Perséphone*.

Schwerké, Irving—Stravinsky's Perséphone. *In* Musical Courier. Vol. 108, no. 21, pp. 5, 20. New York, May 26, 1934.
Note on the Ida Rubinstein production of this work in Paris.

A Stravinsky Manifesto. *In* The Musical Times. Vol. 75, p. 814. London, Sept. 1934.
An extract from the composer's statement on *Perséphone*. Published in full in Le Monde Musical, May 1934.

PETROUCHKA

Barnett, David—Petrouchka, an Analysis. *In* Fortnightly Review. Vol. 1, no. 4, pp. 3-5. New York, Feb. 1928.

Beaumont, C. W.—The Diaghilev Ballet in London: A personal record. London, 1940.
Contents include: *Petrouchka*, pp. 41-50.

Beaumont, C. W.—Petrouchka, decorated by Michel Sevier. London, Beaumont, 1919. 16 pp. Illus.

Benois, Alexandre—Reminiscences of the Russian Ballet. Translated by Mary Britnieva. London, Putnam, 1941.
Contents include: *Petrouchka*, pp. 322-338.

Calvocoressi, M. D.—Ballets Russes. *In* Comoedia Illustré. Année 3, no. 19, pp. 614-621. Paris, July 1, 1911.
Note and illustrations of first production of *Petrouchka*.

Edgerton, Giles—Petrouchka, Igor Strawinsky's Famous Ballet. *In* Arts and Decoration. Vol. 22, pp. 17-18, 60. Illus. New York, Feb. 1925.

Haggin, B. H.—Stravinsky. *In* The Nation. Vol. 156, pp. 572-573. New York, April 1943.
Note on performance of *Petrouchka* conducted by the composer for Ballet Theatre.

Kleiber, Boris A.—Russisk Ballett. Oslo, Nasjonalforlaget, 1946.
Contents include: *Petrouchka*, pp. 62-71. Illus.

Lawrence, Robert—Petrouchka, a Ballet by Igor Stravinsky, Designed by Alexandre Benois. Told by Robert Lawrence, illustrated by Alexander Serebriakoff. Authorized by the Ballets Russes. New York, Random House, 1940. 39 pp. Illus., music.

Lieven, Prince Peter—The Birth of Ballets Russes. London, George Allen & Unwin, 1936.
    Contents include: *Petrouchka,* pp. 130-153. Illus.
McKinney, Howard D., & Anderson, W. R.—Discovering Music: A course in music appreciation. New York, American Book Co., 1943.
    Contents include: Stravinsky's *Petrouchka,* pp. 231-237.
Martens, Frederick H.—Forthcoming Production of Stravinsky's Ballet Petrouchka, as Staged by Adolf Bolm. *In* Musical Observer. Vol. 18, no. 2, pp. 14-15. Illus., music. New York, Feb. 1919.
Nettl, Paul—The Story of Dance Music. New York, Philosophical Library, 1947.
    Contents include: *Petrouchka,* pp. 322-324.
Petrouchka Given by Ballet Russe. *In* The Opera News. Vol. 7, no. 11, p. 3. New York, Jan. 29, 1916.
    On production at Century Theatre, New York, with Bolm and Massine.
Posner, Sandy—Petrouchka: The Story of the Ballet . . . with decorations by Joyce Millen. London, Newman Wolsey, 1946. 96 pp. Illus.
Rivière, Jacques—Petrouchka, Ballet d'Igor Strawinsky. *In* La Nouvelle Revue Française. Année 3, no. 33, pp. 376-377. Paris, Sept. 1911.
    Critique of first performance.
Schaeffner, André—Petrouchka. *In* Le Ménestrel. Année 93, no. 23, pp. 241-244. Paris, June 5, 1931.
Schaeffner, André—Petrouchka. *In* The Monthly Musical Record. Vol. 62, no. 735, pp. 55-58. London, March 1932.
Scholes, Percy A.—The Ballet Music of Stravinsky's Petrouchka, as played by the Royal Albert Hall Orchestra, conducted by Eugene Goossens. *In* The Gramophone. Vol. 2, no. 8, pp. 283-287. London, Jan. 1925.
Semenoff, Marc—Un Entretien avec Alexandre Benois, ou sur la Manière d'Interpreter Petrouchka. *In* Le Courrier Musical. Année 33, no. 1, pp. 8-9. Paris, Jan. 1, 1931.
Sternfeld, Frederick W.—Some Russian Folk Songs in Stravinsky's Petrouchka. *In* Music Library Association—Notes. Pp. 95-107. Washington, March 1945.
Tomlinson, H. M.—Petrouchka. *In* The Saturday Review of Literature. Vol. 2, no. 19, p. 304. New York, Dec. 5, 1925.

PULCINELLA

Bechert, Paul—Vienna Hears—and Sees—Stravinsky's Pulcinella. *In* Musical Courier. Vol. 90, no. 21, p. 5. Illus. New York, May 21, 1925.
Bertrand, Paul—Ballets Russes. Pulcinella. *In* Le Ménestrel. Année 82, no. 21, pp. 210-211. Paris, May 21, 1920.

Lieberman, William S.—Picasso and the Ballet. *In* Dance Index. Vol. 5, no. 11, pp. 286-291.
　　Notes and illustrations on *Pulcinella.*

Rihouet, Yvonne—Aux Ballets Russes: Pulcinella. *In* La Nouvelle Revue Française. Année 7, no. 83, p. 326. Paris, August 1920.
　　Comment on performance of this work.

Salazar, Adolfo—Pulcinella and Maese Pedro. *In* The Chesterian. Vol. 6, no. 44, pp. 119-125. London, Jan. 1925.

Sales, Raoul de Roussy de—Igor Stravinsky's Pulcinella. *In* The Chesterian. No. 8, pp. 234-236. London, June 1920.
　　Critique of the production in Paris.

RENARD

Bertrand, Paul—Ballets Russes. *In* Le Ménestrel. Année 84, no. 21, p. 239. Paris, May 26, 1922.
　　Note on first performance of *Renard.*

Laloy, Louis—La Musique. *In* Revue de Paris. Année 29, no. 13, pp. 190-191. Paris, July 1922.
　　Critique of *Renard* and *Mavra.*

Lopokova, Lydia—The Russian Ballet at Covent Garden. *In* Nation and Athenaeum. Vol. 45, no. 16, p. 536. London, July 20, 1929.
　　Note on production of *Renard.*

Mangeot, A.—Ballets Russes . . . Le Renard, Mavra. *In* Le Monde Musical. Année 33, no. 11, pp. 215-216. Paris, June 1922.
　　Review of the works.

Rosenfeld, Paul—Musical Chronicle. *In* The Dial. Vol. 78, pp. 259-264. New York, March 1925.
　　Note on the composer's rehearsal of his *Renard* and *Ragtime.*

Schloezer, Boris de—Les Ballets Russes. *In* La Nouvelle Revue Française. Année 9, no. 106, pp. 115-120. Paris, July 1922.
　　Critique of *Renard* and *Mavra.*

LE CHANT DU ROSSIGNOL

Calvocoressi, M. D.—M. Igor Stravinsky's Opera—The Nightingale. *In* Musical Times. Vol. 55, pp. 372-374. London, June 1, 1914.

Chantavoine, Jean—Igor Strawinsky's Rossignol. Uraufführung am der Pariser Gorssen Oper am 26 Mai 1914. *In* Signale für die Musikalische Welt. Jahrg. 72, pp. 939-941. Berlin, June 1914.

H., H.—Igor Stravinsky: Die Nachtigall. *In* Neue Musik-Zeitung. Jahrg. 46, no. 19, pp. 455-456. Stuttgart, July 1925.

La Guardia, Ernesto de—El Ruisenor de Igor Strawinsky. *In* La Revista de Musica. Ano 1, no. 2, pp. 18-21. Buenos Aires, August 1927.
Note on *Le Chant du Rossignol.*

Moreno, H.—Ballets Russes: Le Rossignol. *In* Le Ménestrel. Année 80, no. 23, pp. 178-179. Paris, June 6, 1914.
Review of first performance.

Morris, R. O.—Beecham Opera; The Nightingale. *In* The Athenaeum. No. 4674, p. 1265. London, Nov. 28, 1919.
The writer comments, "Whenever anything more than technique is required, Stravinsky's failure is nakedly complete."

O., S.—The Russians at Drury Lane. *In* The English Review. Vol. 17, no. 68, pp. 561-564. London, July 1914.
Includes brief estimate of *Le Rossignol.*

Prunières, Henry—Igor Stravinsky's Chant du Rossignol. *In* The Chesterian. No. 9, pp. 271-274. London, Sept. 1920.
On the Paris production with choreography by Massine.

Rivière, Jacques—Le Saison Russe: Le Rossignol, opéra en trois tableaux d'Igor Strawinsky, après le conte d'Andersen. *In* La Nouvelle Revue Française. Année 6, no. 67, pp. 150-159. Paris, July 1914.
Critique of first performance of this work.

Rivière, Jacques—Les Ballets Russes à l'Opera. *In* La Nouvelle Revue Française. Année 7, no. 78, pp. 463-467. Paris, March 1920.
Critique of performance of *Le Chant du Rossignol.*

Le Rossignol. *In* Musical Courier. Vol. 92, no. 10, pp. 5, 45. New York, March 11, 1926.
Note on performance at the Metropolitan Opera House.

Schloezer, Boris de—Le Rossignol de Strawinsky au Pleyela. *In* La Revue Musicale. Année 4, no. 3, pp. 168-169. Paris, March 1923.

Stravinsky, Igor—Die Nachtigall. Lyrisches Märchen in drei Akten von Igor Strawinsky und S. Mitusoff, nach Andersen. Deutsche Ubersetzung von A. Elukhen und B. Feiwel. Berlin, New York, Russischer Musikverlag, 1923. 20 pp.
Libretto. German text.

Stravinsky's Opera in London. *In* Opera Magazine. Vol. 1, no. 6, p. 27. New York, June 1914.
Note on performance of *The Nightingale.*

Turner, W. J.—The Nightingale and the Immortal Hour. *In* The New Statesman. Vol. 20, no. 500, pp. 178-179. London, Nov. 11, 1922.
A critique of this work.

Turner, W. J.—Stravinsky and Scriabin. *In* New Statesman. Vol. 14, no. 346, pp. 220-221. London, Nov. 22, 1919.
Comment on *The Nightingale.*

LE SACRE DU PRINTEMPS

Beaumont, C. W.—The Diaghilev Ballet in London: A personal record. London, Putnam, 1940.

Contents include: *Le Sacre du Printemps*, pp. 72-76.

Blanche, Jacques-Emile—Les Russes. Le Sacre du Printemps. *In* Revue de Paris. Année 20, no. 23, pp. 517-534. Paris, Dec. 1, 1913.

Blom, Eric—Stravinsky—The Rite of Spring. *In* The Music Teacher. Vol. 10, no. 1, pp. 25-26. London, Jan. 1931.

Calvocoressi, M. D.—Critique Musicale du Sacre du Printemps. *In* Comoedia Illustré. Année 5, no. 17. Paris, June 5, 1913. (Supplément artistique . . . saison des Ballets Russes.)

Calvocoressi, M. D.—Musicians Gallery: Music and ballet in Paris and London. London, Faber & Faber, 1933.

Contents include: Note on Stravinsky's *Rite of Spring*, pp. 221-225.

Casalonga, Marguerite—Nijinsky et Le Sacre du Printemps. *In* Comoedia Illustré. Année 5, no. 17. Illus. Paris, June 5, 1913. (Supplément artistique . . . saison des Ballets Russes.)

Cocteau, Jean—Le Coq et l'Arlequin. Notes autour de la musique. Paris, Editions de la Sirène, 1918.

Contents include: Fragments d'Igor Stravinsky et le Ballet Russe, pp. 60-62.—*Le Sacre du Printemps*, pp. 62-69.

Dent, E. J.—Le Sacre du Printemps. *In* Nation and Athenaeum. Vol. 29, pp. 445-446. London, June 19, 1921.

Garcia Morillo, Roberto—La Consagracion de la Primavera, de Igor Strawinsky. *In* Boletino Latino-Americano de Musica. Año 4, no. 4, pp. 193-219. Montevideo, 1938.

Gray, Cecil—The Sacre Re-heard. *In* Nation and Athenaeum. Vol. 44, no. 18, pp. 616-617. London, Feb. 1929.

Georges-Michel, Michel—Ballets Russes, Histoire Anecdotique. Paris, Aux Editions du Monde Nouveau, 1923.

Contents include: Les deux *Sacre du printemps*, pp. 47-50.

Gilson, Paul—Le Sacre du Printemps. *In* La Revue Musicale Belge. Année 1, no. 12, pp. 1-4. Brussels, April 1928.

H., C.—Stravinsky at the Queen's Hall. *In* The Spectator. Vol. 126, p. 779. London, June 18, 1921.

On a performance of *Le Sacre* conducted by Koussevitzky.

Hale, Philip—Le Sacre du Printemps. Boston Symphony Orchestra program. Forty-third season, 1923-4. April 11, 1924. Pp. 1559-1568.

Hutchinson, Hubbard—Music: the Composers' League Presents. *In* The Nation. Vol. 130, pp. 605-606. New York, May 21, 1930.

Note on a performance of *Le Sacre* at the Metropolitan conducted by Stokowski.

Kalisch, Alfred—London Concerts. *In* The Musical Times. Vol. 62, pp. 488-489. London, July 1, 1921.
Review of concert performance of *Le Sacre* conducted by Goossens.

Lalo, Pierre—Remarks on the Ballet, Le sacre du Printemps. *In* New Music Review. Vol. 12, pp. 440-443. New York, Oct. 1913.
Review of the ballet from Le Temps, translated by Mrs. Daniel Gregory Mason.

Laloy, Louis—Le Sacre du Printemps. *In* S.I.M. La Revue Musicale. Pp. 45-46. Paris, May 1, 1914.

Program of Le Sacre du Printemps for League of Composers. New York. The League of Composers and the Philadelphia Orchestra Association present Igor Stravinsky's *Le Sacre du Printemps* . . . under the direction of Leopold Stokowski . . . April 22, 1930. 12 pp. Illus.
Program contains scenario of this work.

Mangeot, A.—Le Sacre du Printemps. *In* Le Monde Musical. Année 25, no. 11, p. 176. Paris, June 15, 1913.
Review of the first performance.

Moore, Douglas—From Madrigal to Modern Music: A guide to musical styles. New York, W. W. Norton & Co., 1942.
Contents include: Stravinsky—*Le Sacre*, pp. 285-288, music.

Rivière, Jacques—Le Sacre du Printemps. *In* La Nouvelle Revue Française. Année 5, no. 59, pp. 706-730. Paris, Nov. 1, 1913.
One of the first full critiques of this work.

Rivière, Jacques—Le Sacre du Printemps, ballet par Igor Strawinsky, Nicolas Roerich et Vaslav Nijinski (Théâtre des Champs-Elysées). *In* La Nouvelle Revue Française. Année 5, no. 56, pp. 309-313. Paris, August 1, 1913.
Comment on premiere of this work.

Rhodes, Willard—Stravinsky's Le Sacre du Printemps. A critical analysis. Columbia University, 1925. 56 pp., music.
Master's Thesis. Typewritten manuscript.

Le Sacre du Printemps. *In* The Musical Courier. Vol. 100, pp. 7, 15. Illus. New York, March 29, 1930.
Some comments on the work by the composer, Leopold Stokowski and Boris de Schloezer.

Schaeffner, André—Storia e Significato del Sacre du Printemps di Strawinsky. *In* La Rassegna Musicale. Anno 2, no. 11, pp. 536-551, music. Torino, Nov. 1929.

Strawinsky, Igor—Ce que j'ai voulu exprimer dans Le Sacre du Printemps. *In* Montjoie. Année 1, no. 8, pp. 1-2. Paris, May 29, 1913.
The composer's own comments on this work.

Touchard, Maurice—Ballets Russes et Français. *In* La Nouvelle Revue. Tome 8, pp. 117-120. Paris, July 1, 1913.
Note on first production of *Le Sacre*.

Turner, W. J.—The Rite of Spring. *In* The New Statesman. Vol. 17, no. 429, p. 358. London, July 2, 1921.
This work compared with other music of Stravinsky's.

Vernon, Grenville—Modernism in Extremis. *In* The Commonweal. Vol. 12, p. 53. New York, May 14, 1930.
Critique of performance of *Le Sacre* with Stokowski and Philadelphia Orchestra and Martha Graham in principal role.

Vuillermoz, Emile—Le Sacre du printemps. *In* La Revue Musicale. Année 2, no. 4, pp. 161-164. Paris, Feb. 1921.
Comparison of the original 1913 production with the Massine revival.

Vuillermoz, Emile.—La Saison Russe au Théâtre des Champs-Elysées: Le Sacre. *In* S.I.M. La Revue Musicale. Pp. 52-56. Illus. Paris, June 15, 1913.
Comment on the first performance of this work.

SYMPHONIE DE PSAUMES

Cottler, Joseph—Stravinsky's Testament. *In* Disques. Vol. 2, no. 8, pp. 334-336. Philadelphia, Oct. 1931.
Note on *Symphonie de Psaumes*.

Darrell, Robert—Ecstasy Without Grimace, a Review of Stravinsky's Symphonie de Psaumes. *In* Phonograph Monthly Review. Vol. 6, pp. 6-7. Boston, Oct. 1931.

Olivier, Francois—Symphonie de Psaumes d'Igor Strawinsky. *In* Le Monde Musical. Année 42, no. 3, pp. 85-87. Paris, March 1931.

Pilkington, Vera—Stravinsky and Walton. *In* London Mercury. Vol. 25, no. 147, pp. 300-301. London, Jan. 1932.
Note on *Symphonie de Psaumes* as performed in London with the Bach choir.

Piston, Walter—Stravinsky as Psalmist—1931. *In* Modern Music. Vol. 8, pp. 42-45. New York, Jan. 1931.
Critique of Stravinskys, *Symphonie de Psaumes*.

Prunières, Henry—Symphonie de Psaumes. *In* La Revue Musicale. Année 12, pp. 78-81. Paris, Jan. 1931.
Comment on this work.

Rosenfeld, Paul—The Two Stravinskys. *In* The New Republic. Vol. 66, no. 846, pp. 20-21. New York, Feb. 18, 1931.
Note on the *Capriccio* and *Symphonie de Psaumes*, turning points in the composer's career.

Sacred Themes in the Modern Idiom: Stravinsky's Symphony of Psalms. *In* The British Musician. Vol. 7, no. 12, pp. 257-261; Vol. 8, no. 1, pp. 10-18. Birmingham, 1931.